The Ever-Loving Shepherd
and
The Small Lamb

WHITE ROCKS PUBLISHING
POST FALLS, IDAHO
ISBN: 978-1-7322327-6-1

By Udi Merioz, Israeli Artist

Udi Merioz was the curator of the Israeli Prime Minister's Art Collection and is the owner of The Blue and White Art Gallery in Jerusalem. He is a graduate of the Edinburgh College of Art. In 1976, he created the artwork for the 200-Year Celebration of the Independence of the United States, part of the collection of President Jimmy Carter which is now hanging permanently in the White House. In 1979, Udi was commissioned by the Israeli Air Force to create an artwork to commemorate the Peace Treaty between Israel and Egypt.

Udi's father, Elyada Merioz, was the first Jewish person to resettle in the Old City of Jerusalem. Elyada opened the Blue and White Art Gallery in the middle of the Jewish Quarter, just days after the Six Day War in 1967. Now, Udi (and his cat Lo-Sheli), steward the Blue and White Art Gallery, welcoming anyone who walks by and visits.

Udi and John initiated a good and lasting friendship back in 2016 and have maintained connections since. It is an honor and blessing to be allowed the use of this very special painting as the cover for this book.

And a warm thank you Sam Parigi for sharing as well.

The Backdrop to the Cover Picture – *You Raise Me Up*
(via email from Udi):

My daughter arrived at the gallery in a storm of emotion, so I sent a message to my wife.

"Did you talk to her?" she asked.

"Talk to a volcano?" I replied, and promptly sent her a little sketch:

My wife, though not a painter, sent my painting back to me with a small adjustment and a note.

**"Sometimes a volcano is just a little lamb that desperately
needs some attention and love."**

I waited a bit, spoke with my daughter, listened to what was bothering her, and watched as she calmed down. Then I picked up my brushes and painted my next piece…You Raise Me Up.

Thank you Udi for sharing this wonderful story and the blessed inspiration from it. May the Lord continue to shine His face upon you and your family, Shalom…your dear friend, John.

The story of…

THE EVER-LOVING SHEPHERD
AND
THE SMALL LAMB

By Rev. John Young

Edited by Wendy Saxton and Arianna Padula

WHITE ROCKS PUBLISHING
POST FALLS, IDAHO

Acknowledgements:

The Holy Spirit of God inspires and moves. I thank the Holy Spirit for everything He gives. Thank you Father, for sending the Son. Thank you Jesus for sending the Holy Spirit – My Helper, my Counselor…

This work could not have been done without recognizing key people who I've walked life with and who've helped define the need for making purpose to write such things.

For my wife Kim and her diligence to being such a good and faithful servant – the angel that Jesus sent for me. My daughter, Karlee Joe Young – the gift I never felt worthy of. For my mom and dad whom God so richly blessed me with – a wonderful upbringing, always keeping me in the path of the Lord. For my sister Laura and brother Michael – the awesome sibling bookends to my life.

Pastor Tod Hornby – for making the first outreach and impressing the need to go to Israel. Without this love and effort, we may have never been moved to cross that line and make the pilgrimage. Dan and Sharon Stolebarger (Holy Ground Explorations) – for revealing and experiencing Israel the way we have. Pastor Steve and Verlene Wilson – Our early shepherds within ministry; patient and longsuffering. Craig Flinn – (my earliest youth pastor at Northview Bible Church) for exampling and leading us rag-tags as you did. Great memories – Stand by the Power!

Mindy, Renee, Melissa, Jordan, Amanda and many other great people I have been honored and privileged to serve alongside and learn from.

And a final thank you to Wendy Saxon - for your editing work that brought insightful feedback, dedication and diligence to this offering (any mistakes are still mine). And to my biblical editor (and cherished student) Arianna Padula - for your faithful work and devoted commitment to such an important task.

To friends in Israel:

Erez (my brother afar), Tal, and Bar. Thank you for all the kindness and for allowing us to have such special times and great memories with you…(and Pollo).

Udi (and Lo-Sheli). Thank you for each and every moment we've spent with you. You are a dear man who has left the most beautiful painting upon our hearts…

Dedication

As in all things, may this bring glory to our Lord Jesus Christ...
My Good and Ever-Loving Shepherd

And to my dearest friend Kevin "Nesia" Malarkey. You filled the darkest voids in my hardest days and most difficult isolations. You made me feel loved and wanted in times when there seemed anything but. You reminded me to enjoy the laughter's of life through countless hours of ice-fishing, loosing lures, and bucket launches. We had times live...

Top O' the morning Nesh...

Table of Contents

Forward

Forward

Over many years after fully returning to a walk with Christ, I now feel compelled to share some of the experiences that have formed much of what He has stirred within me since. When we course through a lifespan of peaks and valleys that offer real-world examples of victories and defeats, it is well-intentioned to share them with a hope to uplift and help others. We should all want to warn others of possible traps that may lie ahead within our footpaths. It's what a proficient guide does, regardless of field or profession. They glean the wisdom from experiences and become better guides upon each and every leading thereafter. Maybe it's better said as, "Do as I say, not as I did" kind of thing.

Our memories are as equally valuable when used in this regard. More often than not, when memories are shared, you'll find they're usually wrapped with some nugget of wisdom and knowledge. Not semantics. Wisdom and knowledge are different. But they seem most effective (and effectual) when working in tangent with one another. So operative in effect, they became the core to one of the greatest answers ever given.

One night, God appears to King Solomon and allowed him to ask for anything (1 Kings 3:5; 2 Chronicles 1:7). King Solomon wisely asked for a heart of wisdom that would bear the

I

knowledge of discernment, and the understanding of justice in order to lead God's people the best way possible (1 Kings 3:9; 2 Chronicles 1:10). Not only did God grant Solomon wisdom and knowledge, God also gave him great wealth, riches, and fame; the things he could have asked for but didn't (v.11-12). In sum, Solomon was the wisest man to ever have lived. He shared his knowledge and wisdom.

When I look back and reflect upon my days of wonton recklessness and irresponsible actions, I often wondered why the Lord spared me as He did. I say "spare" because that's the most accurate reflection of my outcome to date. In my lowest of lows, I attempted to take my own life and end what I believe to be nothing worth living for. The details don't necessarily matter now, but the result was monumental. Obviously, I survived. But in all fashion of practical reality and the laws of physics, I shouldn't be here.

For decades, I wrestled with the "why" of being spared. And for many years after, I really didn't want to be. But herein is the love and mercy of God. It's not cliché. He had plans for me, and He wasn't giving up on them. In fact, His plans were much bigger than me, and they weren't about me, but they somehow needed me.

I've come to realize that many of the questions about life and our navigations through it don't get answered until the Lord feels were ready to actually hear them. And not only hear them, but are willing to accept them for His will and His purpose, not ours. Understand, some answers will be saved for later, but those necessary to continue serving Him will become evident in His perfect timing. It's all about perspective and position. Choose this day whom you will serve (Joshua 24:15).

As a bondservant of Christ, we are to serve willingly, ably, intentionally, and without reservation or trepidation. A bondservant describes one who gives themselves up to another's will. They are devoted to another to the disregard of their own interests, safety, and well-being. They are those whose service is used by Christ in extending and advancing His cause (and Kingdom) among mankind. So, are you a bondservant in heart, soul, mind, and strength? It's a good question to start and end the day with.

This is also my favorite description in serving Him as a legitimately ordained minister.[1] I'm a bondservant of Christ and a Follower of the Way (Acts 9:2; 22:4; 24:14). It's also the reason for His sparing of me that day. Jesus called me to full-time service in 2008. He "broke" my leg and asked me to make a choice at the most important crossroads of life. "Serve Me or serve yourself." I chose the first...

One of the challenges faced in writing is the desired necessity for accuracy (and truth) in representations of what is being written. To this point, the accounts and stories have been given focused attention, specifically to their outlay and details. At times (albeit only a few), efforts to gather information from people in the past sometimes went unanswered. It may be to the fault of our *advanced* forms of communications via the 21st century or it could be the result of old misunderstandings and possible past disagreements. Nevertheless, absent those specifics, the stories are as they are. The real sensitivities are focused more so on things biblical and the things spiritually significant in this sharing.

In turn, many people helped in contribution by filling the gaps or providing further details on past events or certain circumstances. The unexpected blessing was that those that responded to outreach efforts helped heal some wounds, answer some questions, and repair some old relationships.

Finally, this offering is not meant to be raised to levels of perceptive academic examination or primary source material for similar works. Rather, its hope is to be an uplifting and edifying story wrapped within many others. Anything presented that is good and proper is from the Lord. Any failings or errors aside belong to solely to me. A writer for profit I am not, but a prophet natured minister I am. That being said, I hope you enjoy the story of the Ever-loving Shepherd and the Small Lamb…

The LORD is my shepherd: I lack nothing.

Psalm 23:1 (NIV)

Chapter 1 ~ The Memories...

I don't know about you, but for most people there seems to be this serenely type of peace and happiness when we are moved to look back at our first good recollections, **especially those that mark the most special moments in our lives.** It's no coincidence that many are drawn from the earliest of our memories. And even more tend to be those of the life-defining moments that when we think to relive them, they summon deep desires to turnback and go through them all over again. They may even invoke a catching of the breath that gets

1

you all choked up, just like the moment you hit that part in the movie where you look around to see if anyone noticed it got ya.

Many times, these special memory-recalling moments tend to segue into an irrepressible compulsion that mandates the immediate recital to those around you, regardless of the countless times told! Etched in some form of legacy of remembrance, they're the stories that allow us to share memories we hope never to be forgotten. They're the special ones within the special ones.

Maybe these definitive marking times are as early as one running around during a family reunion, sans a diaper, as the multitude gasped in uncontrollable laughter? Possibly the storied awkwardness of holding hands for the first time or the first kiss with your first real crush. Or deeper yet, the butterflied-stirring in the stomach when first falling in love? Maybe it was an achievement that allowed you to standout and feel honored or privileged amongst the many? For mothers, being told they are "with child" and hearing the quick patters of their baby's heartbeat or holding their child for the very first time. For dads, the same.

Without question, some memories are meant to be cherished privately while others are created to be shared over and over again. These are the great-one's grandmas and grandpas recite without fail at each family gathering. We've heard them hundreds of times and yet they always generate the same wide-smiles and funny belly rolls throughout each and every telling.

As I think back, there are times that stood out because they influenced something right at the perfect moment of occurrence. You could liken it to the saying of, "Being in the right place at the right time." Or being blessed "in the moment." Some may say it's luck, but luck is not something a follower of Christ would believe in because our belief is firmly founded in having confidence in what we hope for, and assurance for the things we cannot see (Hebrews, Chapter 11).

Truly, faith is the antithesis of luck. So then, what is the result of faith? Blessing. It's spiritually symbiotic and fully interactive. Interestingly, the original manuscripts of the Bible don't even use the word "luck."[2] The point here is that our special moments are really blessings that are meant with purpose and sometimes, a strong vivid intent. They don't just happen by happenstance. In spiritual terms, they're given to help create waves of compassion, unity, and love within Jesus Christ. And they have specific timings.

These joyful and opportune moments are the manifestations of events that culminate into the blessings of things we hope not to forget. We do not want these treasures to be lost in the same way that many the great recipes of our grandmas have. As generations pass, such things can be neglected. If they're failed to be passed down through tradition or record, they are irreversibly lost. We need to share the memories, and often at that.

My dad used to say, "Timing is everything!" And there are surely times where if we hadn't been standing in that specific place at that specific time, we would have missed something that will never happen again. Just think of maybe seeing a total solar eclipse or the launching of the Space Shuttle at Cape Canaveral, Florida. Rare events for sure. And even more so in respect of the later because the NASA shuttle program has run its course and has been scrubbed altogether. We will never see shuttle lunches again, at least not the way they were. Regrettably, I was never able to experience one in person, but the more I see the past video recordings of those earth-shaking launches, the more I realize that many of us missed out on something truly spectacular.

Alas, these types of events are the breathtaking moments that usually have the same effects on us, especially when we reminisce through them again. They are the especial highlights that tend to define childhood upbringings and mark the trails of our young adolescent milestones. "Ah, the good times…right?" I'm guessing your rolling through some right now…

Regardless, there are very few who can honestly say that they've never experienced a "lifechanging event" or the "moment of moments." But unfortunately, there are some who just haven't had that special experience. In this regard, I'm pretty sure they've never had the gospel shared with them. I say this because for my part, I've never met someone who has come to Jesus and has not declared that specific encounter to be one of the greatest lifechanging events in their life. Here, my prayer is that all believers continue to embrace The Great Commission so we can try to reach the lost and point them in the right direction (Matthew 28:16-20; Acts 1:8). Too many are hurting and needing care of the Good Shepherd. This is an absolute truth that's impervious to time, cultures, generations, or epochs.

So now, "spiritually speaking…
What are your best memories?"

Here again, for countless believers, "the moment of moments" is that day, place, and time they first came to Christ and finally felt the relief of forgiveness from guilt and sin. For others, it may be their public declaration at baptism or a life-testimony before others. Maybe it was witnessing to another who decided to accept Christ Jesus as their Savior right then and there! Point being, there are moments that are just etched within the marble stones of our top-ten lists. And for good reason. Especially those centered around our Lord Jesus Christ.

For myself, I've always known the Lord Jesus. I honestly can't go back early enough to recall I time I didn't. It's been a personal paradox of sorts in that I can't give the time, day, and

5

place where I was saved, but I am. I know countless people who can give the specifics without pause, including my wife Kim, but I can't. I've said prayers over and over, asking and acknowledging Him as my Savior, but I can't remember the first one. Realize though, it's not the specifics in that regard, rather more so the fact I know my faith and belief in Him is what He will declare before the Father (Matthew 10:32; Luke 12:8-9). I know His voice, and He knows mine (John 10:14). He is the Messiah, the Son of God, and my Savior.

I was graciously raised with Jesus and wouldn't have a clue what it's truly like to not know Him. Therein is the enigma of sorts. I don't have the ability to associatively understand the experience of "coming to Christ" like the many who can. But I've learned to look at this as one of several intricate nuances specifically designed for my ability to thrive within His will. I believe He creates us and positions us within the human timeline of history according to His desires for us and in ways that allow us to be the utmost successful. The question is though, are we measuring success through the lens of His eyes or through the planks in ours?

Jesus has amazing plans for us. He sets us in a personally crafted footpath that divinely forms the perfect molding for our abilities to serve Him and His will, if we chose. It's the most important of all aspects within freewill. It's the eternal decision with the utmost consequence. As Joshua declared, "Now, therefore, fear the LORD and serve Him in sincerity and truth; and put away the gods which your fathers served...and serve the LORD...If it is disagreeable in your sight to serve the LORD, choose for yourselves today whom you will serve...but as for me and my house, we will serve the LORD." (Joshua 24:14-15).

Although we stumble, get jammed up, and even hit the bottoms of deep pits, Jesus is never waylaid nor deterred from His desires to see us overcome. Through highs-and-lows, Jesus allows us to be repentful of our sins and seek His mercy (Matthew 3:2; 4:17; Mark 1:15; 6:12; Luke 13:3-5; 15:7). He cultivates character qualities like forgiveness and righteousness for us to edify and nurture (Luke 17:3-4; 2 Timothy 3:16). In full, we learn to serve Him now so we can further our ability to serve Him as Cohen[3] in His future Kingdom (Revelation 5:10).

Even though the specific memory of coming to Christ and receiving salvation has evaded me, I've had an experience with the Lord that could be likened to those who recall that specific time and place they were Born Again. You may even cross a few people similar in circumstance. It's oddly similar to experiences when you tour Israel. It's not necessarily the specific place *where* something happened that's most important, more-so *what* happened. Therein, all believers are unified and share the same. We're forgiven by the Blood...and we're eternally saved! – Amen.

For myself, my standout moment occurred on the first pilgrimage to Israel in 2016, around the seventh-month, on the sixth-day, around the seventh-hour. There were countless incredible places we experienced on this first journey, so to have one stand alone amongst the many is amazing in itself. But it does.

Truly, there are no words to describe one's first time in Israel and not enough space on any page to give it justice. Simply put, you need to go; if you've gone, you know. We now tell first-timers we take to the Holy Land to circle any city, location, or mountain they read in the Bible, and chances are we'll be there! The experience alone is like seeing the Bible transform from black-n-white to full 8K-UHD Technicolor.

Remember watching the original Wizard of Oz? The movie dramatically transforms from the dull blandness of greyscale to the amazing and vibrant colors unveiled in Munchkin Land when Dorthy slowly opens the door after the tornado passed. It was a jaw-dropper! Everything changed dramatically[4] and all our senses were intensely energized. Going to Israel will do the same, but far more because it's spiritual coloring within an authentic illumination. Your Bible will take on an entirely new richness and a whole new life! Again, if you've been, you know.

From several special engagements with the Jewish people to the sacred churches and indescribable picture-book moments, I will always savor each experience we've had in the Holy Land, especially with Adonai's blessing. But on that first precious trip, my spirit was crushed so impactfully, so richly, I can now say with absolute certainty that it was crafted for personal edification and a lifetime of utmost treasuring. In the moment, it was meant just for me, wrapped in the assurance I will never lose it to a flawed or fading memory. It was my spiritually life-defining point of prominence, even beyond my ministerial ordination ceremony and the laying of hands in affirmation and approval. I felt forgiveness delivered personally by Jesus Himself. It was Romans 8:38-39 manifesting around me with overwhelming vividness and an emotional clarity felt deep within.

Israel is awe-inspiring, and it should be no surprise that it was there where I was so intently shattered. Perfectly placed in humility, humbled to where He could restore me anew. Here, I was graciously broken so I could learn to walk again. No more wounds or feelings of guilt from past sins and regrets.

There are countless incredible places in the Holy Land, but very few sites are certain (or without doubts) when it comes to the exact places where Jesus was, or where He did something as recorded in Scripture. For example, the Baptism Site "Bethany beyond the Jordan" (Al-Maghtas), located in the Jordan Valley, just north of the Dead Sea, is commonly accepted as the location where Jesus of Nazareth was baptized by John the Baptist.[5] But, it may not be the exact spot. Could be up the Jordan a Sabbath day's walk, or downriver the same. Equally, the burial site for Jesus is still weighed between the Church of the Holy Sepulchre and The Garden Tomb. No real certainty. It could be one or the other. And there are still divisions hinged on deep emotions hardened with centuries of viable arguments that cross people today.

The Pavement and the Pit, where Jesus was scourged and later left abandoned (Psalm 88), is thought to be in Gallicantu outside the Old City. "The prisoner's cell (the Pit) offers a sobering insight into where Christ might have spent the night before He was crucified. It has become known as "Christ's Prison"".[6] It's hard to "tour" such a site because it stirs many hard emotions (just think of the 2004 movie *The Passion*). But in terms of specifics, we are not 100% certain that this spot within The Church of St. Peter, in Gallicantu, was the cell where Jesus was held after His brutal flogging. In whole, there are very few places we can truly say "Jesus was right here" when it comes to Israel and places beyond. So the question is this - Is it more important to be in the exact place where something happened, or more fitting to understand the "what" of what happened? I lean the later.

But there are a few places we can be certain that Jesus was there. The Southern Steps, cornered just to the southeast of the sacred Western Wall within the Old City is certainly one (the stone seating within Synagogue at Magdala is also another). I've been privileged to have several visits to the Steps. It's also the site where the world's most famous astronaut Neil Armstrong made a most humbling statement for a man of his stature. When he walked the site, Armstrong professed, "I am more excited stepping on these stones than stepping on the moon."[7] Armstrong declared his moment at that specific site to be the one of the greatest moments of his life (and he was the first human being to step foot on the "lesser light"). Why Armstrong's decree? It was because Jesus was there for certain (Matthew 12:25; John 7:14; 28, 8:20; 18:20). What a profound example of defining the moment and putting things in a sharpened perspective focused directly on Christ first!

I've witnessed the Tomb at the Garden (it's still empty), viewed the Church of the Holy Sepulchre, walked the soothing shores of the Galilee, and been humbled to preach at the Mount of Beatitudes. But it was at the Garden of Gethsemane that Yeshua brought me to my knees in the hardest, deepest, and most loving way. Why? It was here that the Son of God also prayed for mercy (Matthew 26:36-46; Mark 14:32-42; **Luke 22:39-46**). I desperately sought it as well.

The Garden of Gethsemane is located across the Kidron Valley from the Old City of Jerusalem at the base of the Mount of Olives. The Garden is basically sectioned off with free access areas and then other places that are fenced for privacy that must be reserved in advance in order to access them. This is done to allow the masses of tourists the ability to experience parts of the Garden without a tour guide or special privilege, yet also afford larger groups private time for devotions, short teachings and preachings, or just time to humbly reflect.

On our first tour with Dan and Sharon Stolebarger of Holy Ground Explorations, we were able to have a special private time in the reserved area. Truthfully, without Dan and Sharron's decades of nurturing relationships and endearing love towards Israel and her people, we wouldn't have had many of the most special experiences that God has blessed us with while in the Land. Many others can testify the same.

After a short teaching and provisions to worship collectively within the private area of Gethsemane, we were dispersed for the remainder of our hour's allocation. My wife and I left our group still holding hands, then turned our gazes and drifted apart to separate ways within the Garden. We both wanted private time in this most awe-inspiring of places.

The area we had allotted to us was interspersed with the famous, grand old crookedly-type olive trees and the surrounding ground was simply of dirt, scattered rock, couple of native flowers here and there, and a few varied stones. It was hazed with dust and lightly strewn with natural debris throughout. Not necessarily what one would expect for such a treasured landmark location with the name garden in it. But it

12

was here that I entered a spiritual experience beyond surreal, even supernatural.

I remember looking around for a quite spot, away from others, where I could simply sit down, pray, and maybe do a little reflecting. Measuring the available areas and seeking a good landing, I identified in the distance a lowly tree that seemed to be my lot. Kim faded off to another part of the Garden, and I sat down to settle in. I could instantly feel the edged rocks and rough ground beneath me for this place I chose to sit, and it felt proper to be here. It knew it was where He wanted me, but I had no idea the real pull as to why. Physically, it was already a tinge uncomfortable and even painful to sit on the hardened soil. Yet these somatic sensations would soon be overtaken by an overwhelming spiritual presence. Something was manifesting outwardly that started churning emotions inwardly, and it wasn't gradual in its impacting affect.

The olive tree I chose was not as grand in standing stature as the others around it. And it surely wasn't like the ones we often see in the famous paintings of Jesus praying to Abba Father. Ironically, some of the famous paintings we see tied to Christianity are nothing close to an accurate portrayal of what it was really like. Sorry friends, but Da Vinci's Last Supper was a pretty big miss in this regard, intended or not. First, the disciples were not old men with grey hair and long grey beards, forty-years beyond Jesus' age. They were boys and young men.

Second, they didn't eat sitting upright at a table, they reclined (Matthew 26:7; Luke 7:36; 11:37; 22:14; 24:30; John 12:2). While there are more examples of why Da Vinci's missed the mark if he was trying to be even close to accurate, suffice it to say, the painting does not bode well for all things authentic or true. Moreso artistic freedom or license within the spirit of Catholicism and the Hellenistic offerings of those times.

In sum, the tree that caught me was not arched in perfected moonlight with a majestic stone serving as the altar such as portrayed in Heinrich Hofmann's famous painting.[8] It was more so simple, not a stand-out by any means. But it seemed to be where Yeshua and I would meet in a deep sequestered intimacy.

As I sat with my back up against the modest, scraggly looking olive tree with only a few netzers[9], I slowly dropped my head in my hands and began to pray. Looking down at the dust beneath me, I just started weeping. My mind became intensely focused because I knew He was here in this very place before, and this very ground received His sweat, blood, and tears as He prayed to Abba Father the night of His arrest (Matthew 26:36-46; Mark 14:32-42; Luke 22:39-46). And what started as soft crying within my prayer, turned into heavy tears that dropped down and began to form pools of lightened mud. I began trembling uncontrollably within my pleas for forgiveness.

I sensed the presence of the Lord in a way I have never experienced before. I felt the cries and petitions of Yeshua as He pleaded for the cup of wrath to be passed (Matthew 26:29; Mark 14:36; Luke 22:42-44). I was living through the moments and feeling the stripes of what my sins did to Him. He paid the price of that which I could not, and I felt this with a deep cutting agony and indescribable remorse. I just couldn't stop saying I was sorry. *Seventy times seven* didn't seem to be enough.

Losing track of time, Kim came over and started to console and comfort me, but it really didn't take at the moment. I had no idea how hard I was trembling. Her timing was perfect. But it wasn't too long before she started crying alongside, fully emersed in the grieving I was experiencing. With my wife's hand on one shoulder, I felt Jesus's hand on the other. I was immediately consoled and became calm within His reassurance and comforting. It was Him…

Even though forgiveness was already given on the Cross thousands of years before, it was here that I felt the fullness of His mercy and love. I too wept. I just wanted to say sorry. And while this may seem heavy, even somewhat surreal, it was genuine. His mercy is always operative, and at all times, even if it seems hidden. This was the moment He crafted especially for me. It was my associated feeling of coming to Jesus for the first time. It became my time and my tree of weeping.

I was so blessed to share that with Him, and with Kim. And even though it wasn't my first experience with Jesus, it undoubtedly was something meant to be treasured as the most special. But even more so, it is something I continually reflect upon in devotion to the devastating impacts of my sins upon Him. My actions cost the Son of God His life. Yours did too. That's not meant to make you feel bad per say, but being guilty of something and having someone else take the penalty should deeply cut the heart of those who believe. The price was heavy (1 Corinthians 6:20).

Graciously, the Son became the sacrificial Lamb (John 1:29, 36; Revelation 5:6; 6:1; 7:9-10, 17; 12:11; 13:8; 14:1; 15:3; 17:14; 19:9; 22:1, 3). And although sin is forgiven when we faithfully confess it before Him (1 John 1:9), we must remember the consequences of them and not just cast them aside as already paid for.

This too is part of my love and adoration for our Lord. He's always been forgiving and abundantly compassionate when we're seeking. Why more people are not seeking the same is why we need to place this upon our daily prayer lists and intentional action plans.

Now, thinking back...Try to remember –

What were your first memories of Jesus?

Perhaps it's part of your earliest of recollections such as being a toddler at Sunday School and singing songs to our Savior! Remember the old felt boards and character stories followed by some kind of snack and juice? Good times when doughnuts or cookies somehow made their way from the main foyer to the Sunday School rooms! Regardless, there's a good chance your first encounter with Jesus is one of the best of the bestest of memories. Jesus tends to do that for us...and quite often at that!

Yet if you haven't had the encounter, in-full, hopefully this book helps highlight the offering to explore Jesus Christ more. If you seek Him, you will find Him. He made the promise Himself:

Ask and it will be given to you; seek and you will find; knock and the door will be opened to you. For everyone who asks receives; the one who seeks finds; and to the one who knocks, the door will be opened.

Matthew 7:7-8 (NIV)

"Tree of weeping" off in the distance to the left.
The Garden of Gethsemane

"Netzers"
The Garden of Gethsemane

Praying at The Southern Steps
Jerusalem

1st Century Synagogue at Magdala
Magdala, Israel

The Jordan River

'Bethany Beyond the Jordan'
Baptism site on the Jordan River
Al-Maghtas

The opening to "the Pit" (aka "Christ's Prison")
Church of St. Peter's - Gallicantu

Photos by J. Young

He maketh me to lie down in green pastures:

He leadeth me beside the still waters.

Psalm 23:2 (KJV)

Chapter 2 - Growing up

It's funny now coming from the perspective of an
ordained minister, but like many kids growing up, I never really
wanted to get out of bed on Sundays and go to church. And it
didn't get any easier during winter. Truly, there wasn't any kid
in the neighborhood who wouldn't give a sworn testimony that
it was totally painstaking to get all dressed-up and breach the
outside cold of Colbert, Washington, just to go to church.
Sledding on Saturday? You bet! That's a whole different story.
But church on Sunday? Ouch!

Mom would ask, "Is it really that painful (even "excruciating") to get dressed nicely and ready for church?!" YES - Absolutely, without a doubt, it really was that "traumatizing!" Dare I say – it really was a stupid question. In fact, I did say that once. And as I'm painfully reminded, it was out loud. Pretty certain I got the wooden spoon for that ill-guided utterance. Can't remember the consequence, but it was either the belt or the spoon. Odds are it was the spoon since it was mom. We were not *spared the rod* in those days (Proverbs 13:24, 19:18). I learned my lessons quickly, and I'm thankful because of it.

Typical of the normal kid in this position, I would not give up the weekly attempt to get out of church without a fight. Every Sunday morning, it was time to *let the games begin!* To properly initiate these confrontations, I would start with the traditional moaning and groaning thing, flavored with a few flailing's of the arms and exaggerated eye-rolls. Just a warm-up to be honest.

Next, I'd move to the ground game. I didn't have much of a repertoire in the early days, so I'd usually start with some tormented rolling on the floor pretending I was being eaten alive by millions of Tasmanian devil-like piranhas or gigantic Amazon fire ants. All this coupled with the fact I was usually half-dressed or still donning my ultra-powerful Aqua-Man pajamas. (ok, so who was your favorite superhero? I chose

24

Aqua-Man because he could ride dolphins and control the fish, just like Jesus did in John chapter 21. I knew that from Sunday School).

Now, if I was truly adamant about my plight, I'd raise the level of my performance. Exacerbation at this stage was just a special seasoning to the pot I was already stirring. Ironically, there seemed to be some reciprocal relationship between the level of my enactments and the lessening of mom's lenience; one that was hinged ever tightly to her subsequent temper. But eventually, they all came to that legendary confluence called *t-r-o-u-b-l-e...Trouble!*

Nevertheless, when it came to trying to get out of something like church, you never gave up until you knew further attempts were only futile and the battle was over. So, continuing the fight, I'd get up and throw in a few thunderous wonton-type stomping's like I was some pork-chopped Godzilla obliterating downtown Tokyo (side note: this performance would also get cut short if I happened to have a few Legos still laying around. You get the picture - even Godzilla is instantly weakened by one of those suckers in the heal)!

All-in-all, quite the display really. But not an act to be carried on too long! Mom's tolerance was about one-minute, twenty-three seconds longer than dad's. Nevertheless, I eventually had this weekly suffering down to a well-orchestrated, Broadway-type performance. To use the parlance of our time, they would'a "gone viral" had they been recorded.

But, they never worked…not even once.

Eventually, after we got to our homebase at Northview Bible Church[10] in the northernmost part of Spokane, Washington, and I started rubbing elbows with my friends, there really was nothing but good times ahead (aside the main sermon service). There was a decent band of kids that populated our little church. On any given Sunday, we would rarely find ourselves without a handful of friends to hang with.

Spokane was home to about 245,000 people in 1974. Not necessarily prominent in terms of cities, but things changed when the famous World Expo took hold of us that same year. Even though we stood in stark contrast to our distant neighbors on the other side of the state in Seattle, our little city was a good place to grow up.

I always looked forward to finding my best friend Craig when we got to church so we could begin the plotting of plans. Soon we'd be off on adventures that usually kept the unwelcomed attentions of our parents and pastors alike! At times he wasn't always able to make it, but we sure embraced the times he could.

I remember one Sunday, Craig really came-through with an ingenious way to counter our moments of boredom and the dreadingly imminent head-nods that always came with the main sermon. We were fully aware that right after the singing we were destined with a burden to try to stay awake during the forthcoming message; dare I say, the most dreaded part of going to church from my perspective.

Staying attentive in church was always a challenge for us kids in those days because we didn't have cell phones or internet back then. So for us, if we could just make it through the adult sermon, we could get to the good stuff in Sunday School and get out of the heavy stuff in the church service. Us kids just didn't seem to work well in the big church. We had to behave, we struggled to stay awake, couldn't sit still, and we didn't understand a lot of what was being taught. And of course, NO RUNNING in the Sanctuary!

Craig Allen Kannberg (aka. "Kannberg") was one of my closest friends growing up. As young kids, we navigated the Mead School district together and were mired in many adventures throughout. We were both short, similar in abilities (especially sports), had the same likes, got a kick at being close friends, and we always wanted to hang-out together. We even purposed to watch the annual Jerry Lewis Muscular Dystrophy Association (MDA) 24-hour telethon[11] every year we could make it work together. I guess you could say we were both strangely compassionate about things like hardships and abuse, especially towards animals. Odd for boys our age I suppose.

Yet even though we were best friends, we didn't live in the same neighborhood. Contrasting from typical cities, our housing developments in North Spokane were spread out over large areas within the school district boundaries. At times, you'd find your best friend (and later on, girlfriends) could live 10-20 miles away, if not more. So, when we had chances to get together outside of school, we jumped on the opportunities. Or to be most accurate, we exploited them.

Craig grew up in a split home, living with his mom Lynn, older brother Brian, and two younger sisters, Kelli and Jill. At the time, I only knew his dad Robert from a distance, but he seemed like a good guy when Kannberg talked about him. They were a good family and treated me well on the few occasions I visited or stayed the night. They lived in a large apartment complex not far from our church. It was located near our high school and a large local shopping center that we road bikes to and hung out at.[12] Pretty cool spot to grow-up if you asked us. We had lots of mountains and forests as opposed to a more traditional suburban outlay.

Kannberg was always laughing, and he had this insatiable desire to be always drawing something. As his drawings and subsequent skills developed, it later served his motivations towards the strong and talented freehand/graphic

28

artist he advanced into. He started with such things like cartoon characters and made-up creations much in the vein of Napoleon Dynamite's "ligers."[13] Soon after, he graduated to independent illustrations of nature and such. He was an incredibly blessed talent. And yes, "was" as in past-tense.

Like so many childhood friends, we lost Craig far too early in life. He passed away on January 5th, 1998, from a gunshot wound in Mesa, Arizona. After we graduated Mead High-School in 1986, I spun away into alcohol and drugs in full measure. My life was soon rutted into off-and-on attendance at Whitworth College (now Whitworth University) while working at a local downtown hot-spot called C.I. Shenanigans. Kannberg and I worked there for a summer season, and then gradually we drifted apart.

Eventually, I lost track of Kannberg and many others. Such wasted days I wish I could get back and repair. In those lost years, I came to find out that Craig fathered two children; a daughter Kelsey, and son named Zack. Craig was a uniquely beautiful soul I will always be blessed to have shared my early years with. Now, just holding tight to what memories remain.

Although my life now as a minister and educator has been blessed beyond, my classmates and I experienced the pains of losing loved ones and friends far more often (and earlier) than what would be considered normal for adolescents of our age. Tyler W., Marty C., Skipper F., Christen G., Kari A., Chad

29

W., Kip M., Colin K., Mike C., Eric L., Heidi W., Lori S., Cameron C., Joe P., Gary D., Warren F., Jeff M., Tina K., Scotty M., Mark G., Billy R., Jenny B., my best friends Joe Goolie... and Kannberg. All uniquely special people who were lost in such short periods of time. Some I was very close to, and some I knew because we were a unified class going through life together and always attached because of it. These are why memories (and the making of them) are so important in our daily undertakings. We don't want to regret not making the Polaroids that are impervious to our fading abilities so affected by time and age. Make the most of building them before you lose the ability to remember them.

For many years in the aftermath of so many losses, I avoided high school gatherings and reunions. What was the point? We were literally having "reunions" every year at someone's funeral. Goolie's was especially hard because like Kannberg, our friendship was special on so many levels. Goolie always protected me (saved my backside more than once during high school football games) and he treated me like a brother. But we saw the path he was on, and even he knew it would be a hard ending. He predicted it.

In all this, it just seemed beyond abnormal for our generation to lose so many, especially in our little corner of the world. Death seemed to devastate and impact our generation more than others. Some say it followed us.

Like Goolie, Kannberg had the ability to make things exciting and fun. But like many of us in those days, he would press the lines of getting in trouble, just to the point of not overstepping or getting caught (at least sometimes). But that one special Sunday at Northview Bible Church, Kannberg unveiled one of the coolest feats of ingenuity I had ever seen. It turned out to be one of the most noteworthy church experiences I've ever had as a young'un.

Sure, like most kids at church we would come up with the little things to keep us occupied during the main sermon like playing tic-tac-toe on the back of the bulletin, or *who can make the person laugh with some stupid face* kinda thing. But this time, Kannberg was going to change everything for us. Yes, history would be made this fine Sunday! How did I know? His cleverly wry smile was always a precursor to the unveiling of something cunningly special.

During the late 1970's, our generation was experiencing the earliest onset of video gaming. Both consoles and handheld units were being created at record paces. Companies like Atari, Mattel, and Coleco were putting out games that were taking our generation by storm. For those who can drawback that far, Pong[14] was the first, and it started it all. Shortly after, QuizKid (the Owl) came out, being one of the earliest handheld products to reach the market. It was a math driven calculator-type game that captivated even the kids who couldn't stand math.

31

This concept of portable, hand-held units then quickly evolved into games like Auto Racing, Electronic Football, Head-to-Head Basketball, Simon, and a few other hugely popular games. Each year they got better and gave us hours of entertainment (they also chewed up countless batteries as well).

Growing up, I had an overwhelming advantage over my friends in this regard. Although our family grew up with very little in terms of money, affluence or family acquisitions, my sister Laura and I were fortunate to have grandparents that owned a toy store in Long Beach, California, called Uncle Al's Toy Corral. Within this rare privilege, she and I had access to all the premier toys we could ever hope for, especially the new have-to-have items and exclusive video games! My younger brother Mike was too young to enjoy this unique benefit, but for Laura and me, it was a special blessing.

So, as our family got to church that one historic Sunday, we settled into our pew-row and I prepared for another monotonous message about some guy named Paul. It always seemed to be about Paul…and that got old for a 11-year-old boy who didn't understand all the big theological terminology. I just wanted to live to be outside somewhere climbing a tree, jumping a bike, playing sports, or skateboarding. This was also why having a church with many windows was beneficial. *(Author's Note: At the time, I really had no idea who the Apostle "Paul" was. I now know I truly missed out on many incredible teachings by the blessed Pastor Glenn Johnson at Northview Bible Church).*

Craig was allowed to sit with us that Sunday, so things were already looking up. Having a buddy to hang with during the adult message always increased the odds of staying awake. And as expected, it also increased the odds of getting in trouble. We only got one warning before we'd get the elbow to the ribs, leg-kick, or stomping-on-the-foot. Those seemed to effectively bring a ceasing to whatever we were doing. Funny, they also came coupled with looks of cringed anger and the crystal-clear impression of a shorter lifespan should we determine to continue on. I can still see those miens of irritation. Hard to say whose was worse, mom or dad's.

After we got through our traditional poking, wiggling, hullabaloos, and irrepressible fidgets, followed by the aforementioned elbow and *the look,* we settled into a measured reasonability of behavior. We always tried to give it a shot. You never knew if good behavior would be rewarded afterwards with a trip to McDonalds or Baskin-Robbins 31-Flavors Ice Cream. Either way, we usually gave some form of a reasonable effort to hold things together.

But who are we kidding here? Self-control in church for a kid can be likened to the words from the great bluesman Jonny Lee Hooker's famous song of 1948 where he writes, *"One night I was layin' down. I heard mama 'n papa talkin'. I heard papa tell mama, "Let that boy boogie-woogie…It's in him, and it got to come out".* (Boogie Chillun) [15] We weren't much different in this respect. Even our parents know we got it in us and soon, the dam's going to break! Some children can sit quietly and behave, while us others have a malfunctioning control mechanism. Only thing I can think of, "It wasn't my fault; it was the control mechanism you gave me Lord…!"

It never took long to reach the point where we were desperately trying to figure out what or how we could improve our chances at staying awake. At least I was. But not old cool-n-calm Kannberg. On this famous Sunday, he already had everything planned out and handled. He was always thinking ahead about those kinda things. And you always knew when he had it figured out because he couldn't hold that infamously wry smile. It was a dead giveaway; like an irrepressible poker-tell.

Moments later (and much to my delight), as I was covertly watching his awkward shuffling, he slowly pulled out a hand-held Coleco Head-to-Head Baseball Game from under his bulging winter coat. Could this really be happening? Did Kannberg really get the game past his mom, past the elders who roam the foyer with eyes like motion-activated x-ray machines, and past the bulletin-bearing guards of the main sanctuary entrances?

I thought he had completely lost all sense of reason and jumped straight into the land of crazy-beyond! I said to myself,

"Are you really going to pull that out and play that in the middle of church? The noise alone will banish us to the dungeons forever! And we all know there are no games allowed in the dungeons – double whammy!" Restrictively flailing my arms the best I could, I started the classic miming act of *"What are you doing???"*

I wasn't as emboldened as Kannberg when it came to certain things like this. Surely not the "guts" to even attempt such a thing. Granted, he was also smart enough to know I was the one sitting closest to the hands that dealt punishment. Admittedly though, Kannberg had wits, ingenuity, and creativity well beyond my abilities. Many of my friends did.

Nevertheless, I couldn't wait to see what would happen when he hit the switch and let 'er go! I remember holding my laughter in, fully captivated by how he's going to pull this one off. It was always something to catalog for a future hangout time so we could marvel at our keenly cunning and master-planning abilities. There's just nothing more satisfying than reliving the best schemes and their successfully orchestrated outcomes. They seem to season better than any of them Picasso's or ramblings by that Shakespeare-dude. We had our own masterpieces, finely crafted in the genuine innocence of the greatest of adolescent young minds. Just ask us.

It didn't take long before my dad saw the game (...parents see everything), but because it was Kannberg and not me, he didn't take the game away. My parents loved Craig because he was a friend who always treated others kindly, had respect for them, and never misbehaved as a guest. Maybe dad also wanted to see what Craig was going to do? I mean dad knew the game would screech and howl with bells-and-whistles the instant he turns it on, so maybe he was as equally curious as I was to see how this was going to unfold...?

Dad was also known as Mr. Young, one of the most beloved teachers to walk the halls of Whitworth Elementary school. I'm not biased. I too was jealous of the students who were blessed enough to get Mr. Young for 3rd Grade. He even taught his students square-dancing. Sounds awkward, but they loved it!

Mr. Young had had a very good reputation and was one of the most requested teachers at the school. He intrinsically knew and loved his kids inside and out, especially my close friends. And later when it came to the girlfriends, he would usually endear them with a nickname as his little quirk of approval. His character qualities are an example I try to follow still to this day. Thinking back, my guess is dad might have been quietly cheering for some measure of creativity and resourcefulness on Craig's part, just to see whatever he cooked up for our church adventure.

Dad allowing Craig to keep the game also was so typical. This type of *double standard* happened quite often. Did you have parents that let your friends get away with stuff right in front of you? It's a tough one, but I figured the good part was that at least my friend wouldn't be angry with me because of something my parents did. Or even worse, have my dad take the game away and make a big-deal out of it later in front of everybody. Dad probably had all that thought out and considered already. Parents have the ability to see what might be best for us, even when we don't recognize it in the moment. It's that wisdom-hindsight thing.

I should never have doubted Kannberg and his resourceful abilities to find a way to get us as close to trouble without getting us into trouble. How did he navigate the sound issues that would surely alert 500+ people and our senior pastor from "our" scheming plan to play video games in the middle of church?

Now, it should go without saying, but I call it "our" plan because once you're aware of the plan, you're in the plan - that's just the rules. But that too also has its problems, especially if…(sorry, better said *when*) you get in trouble. Defending with, "It was their plan…not mine" holds no reprieve. Our parents were children once too; they know the rules and they know the ways to close the gaps as quasi prosecuting attorneys.

Nevertheless, Craig leaned over and quickly whispered the strategy. Apparently, the previous night, he (and I believe his brother Brian) took apart the hand-held baseball game, found the wire to the small speaker inside the device, and skillfully snipped it in two! The game would still play, but with no sound, and it could be fixed again later like it never happened. Back then, games and electronics did not have silencing abilities. Quite the opposite...they were meant to be loud. The workaround was absolutely ingenious on so many levels!

Kannberg hit the power button, lit the game up, and proudly proceeded to play like we all were instantly fitted with soundproof earmuffs. The wry smile he previously had went proudly wide. Eventually I couldn't help it, and before too long, dad saw me try to join the game and that promptly killed the whole deal for me right there. Oh, he allowed Craig to keep playing, but my involvement was clearly over. Although I again had to navigate what I believed to be one of the many unfair things in life, I dealt with it. I sat silently in what seemed like full-body restraints, but inside I was reveling in what my best friend just did. That day, Kannberg beat the system, and I joined in the crowning achievement. It was a smooth move and a prodigious achievement.

Looking back and reflecting, I see Craig as the one small lamb who wondered, while ninety-nine remained back, carefree and safe. We spent decades together, even living together after graduation. We went through heartbreaks, and we went through times I'll never forget. But he seemed to reflect the one sheep that seemed to be left to fall away without pursuit (Matthew 18:12, Luke 15:4). Not necessarily at the neglect of family or loved ones, but rather for reasons that have no real answers. It just seems to seem that way.

It's an empty feeling, helplessness within grief and confusion, when you have so little to go on and little left to hold on to. I know for my part, I feel like I let Kannberg down in the worst ways; much like I let down so many loved ones during those darkened years after high school. I failed the Lord, my family, close friends, and surely myself. Craig Kannberg was a precious soul and an amazingly talented young man.

Maybe Jesus needed a new artist in heaven
the day He took Craig Home...

The infamous Coleco Head-to-Head Baseball Game used by Kannberg during church - circa 1980

But Jesus said, "Let the children alone, and do not hinder
them from coming to Me; for the kingdom of heaven
belongs to such as these.

Matt 19:14

Chapter 3 ~ Finally, Sunday School…I

Not every Sunday sermon experience was met with such childlike musings and calculated schemes like Kannberg and I concocted. Some Sundays we just fought through it because once we got past the main service, Sunday School was waiting! And we loved going to Sunday School at Northview. Like most kids, Sunday School was a good time and good place to be. It also became a place that allowed us to really learn about Jesus in ways we could finally understand.

It only got better as we grew within the church and got older. In my last years at NVBC, I was blessed to have a powerfully energetic youth group leader named Craig Flinn. He was amazing and left many lasting and powerful impressions on me and our small band of believers. He outpoured to us, and we gladly took it all in. He loved on us just as Jesus loved on His young followers. Bet he never thought he'd be raising others in his footsteps. That's one of the many blessings in serving the Lord within ministry opportunities. Seeds get planted and we all wait patiently to see what we hope to become a good harvest. Some may take hold and yield immediate results, and some may not sprout for decades. It's the Living Water of the Lord that will set the germination in action (John 7:38).

Back in April 1976, our church started in an old pizza parlor and steakhouse in the Fairwood Shopping Center called Cisciro's (later Savage House Pizza). We were a church plant from 4th Memorial Church in Spokane. For our onset, this old tavern-like pizza parlor was to be our starting point. As one of several original families, we'd sometimes get there early so Dad and others could cover the pool tables with plywood covers and empty any missed ashtrays from the night before. It was usually dark, but it served our fellowship until we could start our new building. As months passed, the elders found a new property, made plans, and we all started gathering outdoors at the new site each Sunday, even before we broke ground. Didn't take long, but with the blessings of God, and all the volunteer help, we soon completed our church home.

At Northview, our sanctuary was on the main floor of a 2-story building. It was a wood and stone structure set in a rather traditional A-frame architectural-style, with a large foyer that corralled the pre-service gathering rituals of coffee and doughnuts. Unfortunately, food and beverages were for adults-only, except on rare occasions or celebrations. In hindsight, the design of our church was perfect because they stationed the Sunday School classrooms on a lower level in the basement (also good for soundproofing). After the main service, we could make an easy beeline to the stairs and barrel-roll our way into our classrooms like it was some adrenalized variation of Beat-the-Clock while downhill skiing. The stairs were steep, but we knew the patterns well.

The main service had good life to it and was not always the sleeper we begrudgingly anticipated. Our gatherings were very traditional in terms of "church." We began service when the nice elderly lady would start playing the vintage organ while others would approach the steps of the stage. This then signaled everyone to finish conversations, get to your seat, and be ready to start.

I always marveled at how the organist would wave her hands as she played. It was like she was some fancy maestro absent of a supporting orchestra. Somehow in this flowing-type fashion, she could hit the keys exactly at the right time. It was as if she was effortlessly orchestrating butterflies, cuing them to suddenly drop and hit the keys at the precise moment...and then gently rise away. I likened it to watching a harp player smoothly plucking the strings as the musical notes float away effortlessly into a transparent staff-paper waving above.[16] (probably got that from watching Lucy as she annoyed Schroeder on various Charlie Brown cartoons). Our organist was charismatic to watch as she used all those blessed talents leading us in worship. She was good.

We would get settled with general announcements, special notices of upcoming events, and then we'd hit the old Hymns. Mom and dad would always make my sister and me share holding the Hymnbook with them, probably to keep us engaged and paying attention. Do you remember the smell of the old Hymn books? If you can find one today, the scent would still be there. It's a very distinctive and recognizable smell.

Good memories looking up at mom and watching her sing the Hymns as beautifully as she did. Dad not so much. Mom definitely had the upper hand when it came to worship. I liked singing, but I didn't know how to read music or how to stay within the same lines of verses. In fact, the hymn books were confusing to me. Often, mom would use her hand to help me along and keep place. But she knew a majority of the hymns by heart, and soon she'd get lost in her pure love of singing to the

Lord and staying in harmony with the congregation. I never faulted for her forgoing attentions towards looking down and keeping me on track. I didn't mind really, I just enjoyed watching her sing or the organist as she did her waving performances.

At the time, I failed to appreciate the richness and fullness of the traditional Hymns we raised to the Lord during those early years of the 70's. When you contrast those precious early works next to some of today's "worship music," there really is just veiled comparisons. But just as there are many new and wonderfully inspired songs of today that are composed with the purest of intents on glorifying our Lord in true worship, there are just as many doing anything but. Especially under the guise of *Christian Music.*

In this regard, the Lord God deserves our best submissions when it comes to worship, devotion, or anything else we present to him as an offering. Disappointingly, I've seen one too many "worship teams" in today's contemporary churches who are hard-set on tributes geared more-so towards entertaining the masses, self-exaltation, or just shear limelight grabbing. As an example, just watch what a worship team does after their performance. Do they come and join the fellowship of others in the sermon, or do they exit the stage and leave the sanctuary? I see the later more often.

I remember our pastor purposefully waiting for the entire worship team to join their families in the congregations before starting the sermon message. We waited patiently. Though it seems like nothing, I liked it when everyone got together as a church family. It was a good healthy unity that was felt even by us kids. Does it mean that any (or all) worship team(s) are missing the mark if they don't go join the fellowship for the sermon before or after their performance? Of course not. But it means something that some do. Just saying...

The Hymns of Charles and John Wesley, Issac Watts, and even the great Martin Luther, were edifying and inspirational works in many regards. They infused Scripture and spiritual themes, and were purposefully constructed to where the overall focus was not necessarily on the person singing. The intention was steadily on the Lord, as it should be. Using Scripture in music, much like the works of Joshua Aaron (or Aaron Shust from the States), is edifying and enriching to our spiritual health and well-being.

If you are a friend of Israel, you're probably familiar with these two amazing artists. Most of their work is either entirely Scripture or very much interlaced with it. Hard to miss with that type of approach, especially with the entwining of Hebrew within the compositions. Psalms with and within the psalms!

For our fellowship at Northview, we would start by singing 3-4 hymns each Sunday or we would be treated to performances by the church choir. Even though I was somewhat uninterested in church as a whole (weighed heavily because of hard-to-understand sermons), I thought the choir was awesome. They got to wear those cool robes that slowly waved when they walked on and off stage. Dare I say it was angel-like. Plus, when the choir performed, it killed more time. (Yes, I know how bad that sounds, but remember, I was a kid). Anything that chewed up clock was good because it meant Sunday School was inching even closer!

At NVBC, we had Sunday School teachers who could really bring the Biblical Stories to life! You know the ones who could make all the different character voices, sounds, and inflections, as they moved characters on the felt-board or as they displayed some vivid story-board picture. I mean when Daniel got thrown into the lion's den? WOW - Those lions were hunnnnnngry!

I'll never forget when Jonah got shot out of the whale like he came from some bazooka-type cannon! My teacher crescendo'd the whole moment with an epic... "KAAAAAA-BOOOOMMMMM!" And boy did that felt-character Jonah go flying across the room! Nothing but great times and much excitement in living through those treasured Biblical Stories!

But there was nothing like the stories that had Jesus leading the way (and yes, pun intended). Sure, all the other tellings were good as we revisited the biblical heroes like Moses as he leads the Israelites out of the grips of mean-old Pharoh through the Red Sea, or the long-haired Samson tearing apart lions with his bare hands and busting down huge marble pillars! The stories of a young David brazenly wiping out the mammoth-sized Goliath with a little sling and a stone or dodging Saul's flailing spears as he escapes throughout the region of En Gedi, were always inviting and intensely captivating to listen to. It was like we were there, watching first-hand!

But, when the teaching involved Jesus, everything just got so much bigger and much more powerful. He did all kinds of miracles (stuff even superheroes couldn't do), and we did everything we could just to keep our seats. Bring on the Lord Jesus cause aint nothing stopping Him! We just couldn't wait to see what Jesus would do next…

Maybe your first memories of Jesus were when a friend invited you to youth group, Vacation Bible School, or some church camp gathering during which you first learned about God and His only begotten Son. Maybe you stayed the night at friend's house and had-to-go to church when you'd never gone before?

Perhaps a school teacher shared of Jesus and prayed with you to help you through a troubling problem. Back in my days, God had not been removed from public schools, nor prayer, so it wasn't uncommon for those good things to take place – even during the middle of class. I recall more than a few times where my teacher would bring me over to their desk, talk about what was wrong, and offer encouragement as we prayed together. And yes, there was even a hug.

Nevertheless, the stories will surely vary. But the question is this…

What were your first memories of Jesus?

Amazing Grace – Hymn Golden Sheaf 2 #44

Cicero's Pizza & Steakhouse
Northview Bible Church – (1977-78)

Photo: https://northviewbible.church/in-the-archives

Northview Bible Church – (2024)
Spokane, Washington

Photo by J. Young

I am the Good Shepherd; I know My sheep

and My sheep know Me—.

John 10:14 (NIV)

Chapter 4 – "Hey, That's Jesus…"

My earliest memories of our Lord Messiah were seeing pictures of Him as a Shepherd where He was either carrying a small lamb across His shoulders or tending a little one in His arms. These were the pictures around the house, in my first Bible (The Child's Holy Bible, King James Version – with a Cross closer zipper), and the various art illustrations scattered throughout our Church and Sunday School classrooms. But what I didn't realize (at least until it was pointed out) is that some of those pictures and paintings were depicting the little lamb with a wounded or broken leg being cared-to personally by our Good Shepherd as He carried them along. Now as you think back, does this sound like the pictures you saw? Did you notice the lamb had a bandage on a wounded leg...???

Sounds odd, but those first pictures of Jesus carrying a lamb with an injury resonate in my mind like the first time I saw The Spirit of '76 poster (aka: Yankee Doodle)[17] depicting three Revolutionary War soldiers with the Stars and Strips waving proudly behind. One young boy drumming, looking up to an elderly white-haired soldier intensely focused on the same, and the final soldier playing a flute with a bandage on his head. In similar creations following Willard's painting, some dressings were stained red with blood, and some were not.

Regardless, the picture sticks in my mind, drawn mainly by the site of the wound itself. It accentuates the illustration by raising the level of emotional response. When someone is hurt, we tend to respond differently under such conditions, so it has more of a lasting impact. Marketing in business works the same way. Draw on the emotional to lessen or distract from the rational or reasonable. Same effect if you go to an animal shelter looking to rescue an abandoned or unwanted dog or cat. (*I put "rescue" "abandoned" and "unwanted" in the sentence to elevate the reaction to an emotional level.*) Who wouldn't want to save an abandoned animal? When you see these poor animals in cages or behind bars, it's all over – someone's coming home!

Thus, seeing someone or something hurt, evokes a need to respond and do something to help, usually beyond our normal patterns of reaction or response.

Several years ago, while in seminary study at Liberty University, I came across a story that really changed my appreciation of this visual symbolism (for lack of better words). Why was Jesus carrying a wounded lamb? For some reason, I just glossed over the detail specific to the wound and thought Jesus was just being Jesus. I just didn't notice it. Yet, when it was pointed out, I remember feeling a purposeful sense to slow the moment down and take note in consideration. I needed to look and think again. Why the wound?

Stories that tend to be on the edge of being unlikely, unrealistic, or simply embellished fallacies, can either captivate some intrigue or be castoff without a second thought. Yet this one caught attention and deserved to be answered beyond an inquisitive curiosity.

The "story" I came across pointed to a possibility that these pictures of Jesus carrying a wounded lamb may hold something much deeper than what's been previously considered. It's truly an endearing account flavored with the rustic nuance within the oldest of epochs; those dusty days of ancient shepherding in the biblical times of the vast desert wildernesses. And it's intriguing to share to those who may not have heard it before.

But even if you're familiar, there will usually be a different take, spin, or alternative perspective that would allow you to glean something new from it. You can liken it to viewing a chosen movie over-and-over again. Typically, there's something you hadn't noticed before. Something jumps out at you, and often, it's something you make-note to mention to others because it gave you a whole new perspective or altering insight. Either that, or just another blooper like the huge boulders of *Indian Jones and the Raiders of the Lost Ark.* Spoiler alert – look closely…some of the massive boulders bounce!

The point here is that when we cross stories, moments in time, or special instances of noteworthy occasion, we need to stop and take a good pausing. Much like passing by someone you know and asking, "How are you?" Do you really want to know, or is it just a customary courtesy in passing? Stop and listen with intent. Get the true answer to your question. You'll also find that our relationships will be strengthened because it's attention within intention. It shows love and care within the things we will be examined by (2 Corinthians 8:8). Plus, you'll usually hear something you can help pray about.

At the sermon on the Mount as recorded in Matthew 5, Jesus states, ""You have heard that it was said, 'You shall love your neighbor and hate your enemy.' "But I say to you, love your enemies, bless those who curse you, do good to those who hate you, and pray for those who spitefully use you and persecute you" (v.43-44). Did you notice that the Lord does not suspend the command to love thy neighbor? In fact, this teaching was adding more to the first. We are to love our neighbor AND our enemies. Not foregoing one for the other.

We should take a few steps back and make sure we don't overrun special moments and miss some of life's treasures. Especially one's gifted by the Holy Spirit. It could be a spiritual uplifting, a moment of conviction, a time of reflection, a needed rebuke, a cautionary warning, a necessary edification, or just a reminder you are loved deeply and intrinsically by our Abba Father. Whatever the prompting, heed the moment wisely. Slow down and listen to the passerby when you ask how they are doing. Take note of the stranger who may not be a stranger at all (Hebrews 13:2).

Good Shepherd
By Bernhard Plockhorst

The Spirit of '76 (aka Yankee Doodle)
By Archibald Willard

He tends His flock like a shepherd: He gathers the lambs in

His arms and carries them close to His heart;

He gently leads those that have young.

Isaiah 40:11

Chapter 5 ~ The Backdrop

Many of the created pictures of Jesus carrying a small lamb are purposed towards a simple motivation ~ an intentional illustration of the special relationship between the **Good Shepherd and His sheep.** And that within this relationship, Jesus carries the wounded and cares for the weakened. Now, although that may seem somewhat obvious (even simple), there may be something even more-so special to this depiction than what many (like me) had not considered before. In other words - there may be more to the story not meant to be hidden.

At the writing of this book, six times I've traveled the Biblical lands of Israel. I've carefully walked the dusted paths in the Golan Heights, humbly baptized believers in the Jordan River, and joyfully coursed the rocks of the Galilee. I've intently listened to the stones of Jerusalem while devoting on the Southern Steps and I've inserted prayers at the sacred Western Wall. I've seen the waylaid ruins of the **October 7th, 2023,** attacks and the memorial offerings raised in the aftermath. I've come to know (and embrace) Israel as the especial Pasture of God; home to many friends and loved ones I've been humbly blessed to spend time with. I also call it Home now. Prayers go up daily for Erez, Tal, Bar, Este, Moshe, Udi, Daniel, Wassim, Yossi, Eli, Jane, Joshua, Amir, their families, the IDF, and the nation of Israel.

Without question, it can be an overwhelming experience when you make your first pilgrimage to the Holy Land. Whenever asked, I immediately affirm that it is an absolute necessity for each believer to walk and worship in Israel at least once before we dwell there in the future eternal Kingdom (Revelation 21:2). Each follower of Yeshua needs to touch the land, engage with the people, and experience the Scriptures anew by walking the steps of our Lord and Master. Then, to intently witness the experience with others so they too can share in the fullness of her offerings. It is the home of our Good Shepherd, and the Home of our future.

Yet even now as you travel throughout the Holy Land of Israel, you can see and sense the places where shepherds tended their flocks for thousands of years. The rock walls still stand in many places throughout the sloping countryside and valley terrains. You can still see old-rutted pathways and imagine through the steps of those who walked them. The sheep-gates still stand within the weathered stones of the scattered sheepfolds sprinkled throughout the region. They blanket the land with perfecting character and speak intimately to those who long to know the history of the days when Yeshua tabernacled with us.

The land stories its past in deeply ancient ways availed through amazing vistas and panoramas that span the entire landscape. Surrounded with the symphonic sounds from local wildlife and an overwhelming sense of Adonai's presence, it's here that there are no words to describe what it does to the first-time pilgrim. It invokes a deeply peaceful serenity that seizes many respires as it did mine at first gazing. And seeing Jerusalem as you round the corner or crest the hill the first time… inexpressible.

When I first read about this shepherding practice among the shepherds of old, I was pretty taken. No mistaking it was a "wow" type of moment. It seemed hard to believe at first, but it made sense once I had let it sink in as a chanced possibility. And the more I considered it, the more I appreciated its symbolism. Whether true or finely seasoned through time, it captivated my emotions to the point of prayer and personal reflection. Knowing His ways are not our ways (Isaiah 55:8), it surely was something I wanted to explore beyond a superficial searching.

If you've ever read the poem 'Footprints in the Sand' you'll sense the flavor and purpose to such offerings like this story I'm about to share. According to contributors on the Wikipedia, "'Footprints," is a popular modern allegorical Christian poem that describes a person who sees two pairs of footprints in the sand, one of which belonged to God and another to themselves. At some point the two pairs of footprints dwindle to one; it is explained that this is where God carried the protagonist."[18] In its fullness, Footprints is meant to show that the Lord assuredly carries us in the darkest times of our lives, even when we're unknowing and unaware. He's always with us (Matthew 28:20).

These are the type of stories meant to help raise hope and illuminate our understandings on how special our relationship with Jesus is, especially when we are overshadowed with uncertainty, doubts, and difficult sufferings. And for many, those troubled waters may seem constant, if never ending. We call them seasons, but the best part about seasons is that they are supposed to change. Sometimes though, they take far too long, dragging out for what seems like forever. These stories are meant to lift us up when we have fallen into those darkened hardships and those dreadingly drawn-out seasons of overcast and gloom.

Understand, this could be of legend, could be a myth, it could even be a completely made-up tale crafted down through the generations as a great fireside storytelling; one of those anecdotes that unfolds into some morsel of cautionary wisdom or unexpected learning delight.

Alternatively, it could be a simple allegory, even parable-like in nature with an edifying purpose when considered in the full; something given in hopes of shedding a special meaning to take heed in our desires to grow in our relationship with the Good Shepherd. There's the possibility it's also intended as instructionary within the spirit of truthful oral traditions, much like those of the Biblical times. Maybe a singular-type treasure to add to the multitude of understandings that allows us to see God's perfection in His divine lovingkindness, and the intrinsic value He holds within each individual life...like that of the shepherd to his sheep.

Here, to each their own interpretation and meaning for sure. But, for lack of better words, you and the Holy Spirit get to unpack this one.

Personal footprints in the sand
Newport, Oregon

Photo by J. Young

Save Your people and bless Your inheritance;

be their shepherd also, and carry them forever.

Psalm 28:9

Chapter 6 ~ The Chronicle

From the earliest days of recorded history, shepherding was given prominence in the human task. In fact, it was "the" task. Consider this, although the first command of mankind was to, "Be fruitful, and multiply, and replenish the earth, and subdue it: and have dominion over the fish of the sea, and over the fowl of the air, and over every living thing that moveth upon the earth" (Genesis 1:28, KJV), the first duty chronicled in Scripture was for mankind (Adam) to care

71

for the flora and fauna in the Garden (Genesis 2:15). We can then draw to Abel who was the first specifically declared "keeper of the sheep" (Genesis 4:2). It's also why Cain flippantly remarked, "Am I my brother's *keeper?*" (Genesis 4:9). Yes, yes you were…

Did you ever consider that the first person murdered was indeed a shepherd? Arguably, this could be one of the earliest foreshadowings of Jesus and His crucifixion, although clearly distinguished apart on several points. The similarity to consider? - They were both shepherds who were murdered.

To chronicle further, after the first shepherd Abel, we have Abram & Lot (Genesis 13:5). We then read of Isaac (Genesis 26:14) and the herders of Gerar (Genesis 26:20), and the shepherdess Rachel (Genesis 29:6, 9) and Jacob, Laban (Genesis 29:10) and then Esau (Genesis 33:9). Yes, these notable biblical figures were all shepherds and we're not even through the First Book of Torah.[19] Safe to say that most people mentioned in the beginning were shepherds.

We then have Zipporah (Exodus 2:16), Moses in Midian (Exodus 3:1), a young David who later became king (1 Samual 16:19; Ezekiel 34:23), his son King Solomon (1Kings 4:20-28; Ecclesiastes 2:4-7), Cyrus the Great (Isaiah 44:28), the prophet Amos (Amos 7:14), on down to the blessed shepherds who were told of the "good tidings and great joy" on that precious night of Jesus' birth (Luke 2:8).

There were countless shepherds of renown and even more so unknown. In sum, there is no mistaking, shepherding is referenced throughout the Scriptures, from Genesis to Revelation, and it is with His intention to be so. It's the model given us in terms of caring for each other - loving thy neighbor as you should love yourself, but also praying that love will overcome our enemies as to draw them to the salvation of Jesus Christ (Leviticus 19:18; Matthew 5:43-44).

In reflection, I'm reminded of passages that point to the divine ways God brings forth His special announcements, commands, and prophecies. Many of His interactions with mankind and the rest of Creation are revealed regularly through unexpected and unique means (Isaiah 55:8-9). These are also some of the epic go-to points of the Scriptures that form many of our essential understandings in doctrines and the covenants bestowed. But for the reader here, key-in on the people who He unveiled these special announcements to, including those He used to fulfill them as His vessels of divine grace.

No mistaking the intention of selecting the humble and the unknown, and especially those deemed unworthy during those biblical times (i.e. women, outcasts, slaves, the simple-tongued, foreigners, the second-born, prostitutes, fishermen, tax collectors, gentiles, Roman centurion's, leppers ...and yes - lowly shepherds of the fields).

Consider the Old Testament:

- Although God spoke all things into existence through His Son Jesus Christ (Colossians 1:16), the woman Eve was the first thing He made by His very own hand (Genesis 2:21~22) ~ Read it closely! Set apart from all other parts of Creation, she was created special... Handcrafted by God!

- God destroyed all living things on the earth (Genesis 7:21~23), sans the eight and the animals they stewarded (Genesis 7:7), and gave us the rainbow as a covenant promise (Genesis 9:13~16). Imagine the things they saw and endured, especially the moment they gazed upon that special covenant *sign* that was set above a gleaming new earthly landscape. At God's command, the waters receded, and they soon saw a whole new earth. Bet it was welcomed words when they finally heard the command to exit the Ark (Genesis 8:16)! Here, just one family started it all over again.

- God displayed His power over all things (including the false gods of Egypt) with the Ten-Plagues. And with that, the ungifted orator Moses was front row for it all. Eventually, his choice was not to have a choice.

- A well renowned prostitute named Rahab turned Biblical heroine for sparing God's spies (Joshua 2). She had quite the hand in the unfolding of God's plans…she and countless other prominent women in the Bible.

- Cyrus the Great was a great shepherd of the Jewish people who was not of the Jewish people. He was a Persian king.

And the New Testament:

- Who was the first recipient of the divine pronouncement that a Savior would be born?

    - *It was Mary, not Joseph!*

    Luke 1:30-31…

    The angel said to her, "Do not be afraid, Mary; for you have found favor with God. "And behold, you will conceive in your womb and bear a son, and you shall name Him Jesus.

- Who was the first person to worship Jesus? A guy who would grow up eating bugs and wearing camel skins. He was the path-preparer and cousin of the Messiah.

    - *It was John the Baptist!*

    Check Luke 1:41…

    When Elizabeth heard Mary's greeting, the baby leaped in her womb, and Elizabeth was filled with the Holy Spirit.

- Who was the first to see the resurrected Jesus?

    – Not the Twelve!

Now when Jesus was risen early the first day of the week, He appeared first to Mary Magdalene, out of whom He had cast seven devils ~ (Mark 16:9)

It was Mary Magdalene, and Joanna, and Mary the mother of James, and other women that were with them... ~ (Luke 24:10)

- Who heard the Angels first herald that precious Holy Night that Emmanuel came? **– The lowly shepherds of the Judean Hills.** Not the High Priest or Pharisees in Jerusalem, and surely not the audience we would have expected for the Greatest Announcement ever to be made in human history.

In the same region there were some shepherds staying out in the fields and keeping watch over their flock by night. And an angel of the Lord suddenly stood before them, and the glory of the Lord shone around them; and they were terribly frightened. But the angel said to them, "Do not be afraid; for behold, I bring you good news of great joy which will be for all the people

    (Luke 2:8~10)

Those shepherds were special because they were not special among men -they were divinely chosen.

Our Savior had this special association with shepherds for countless reasons that theologians will pose and position until the Second Coming. Rightly so. There's nothing wrong with seeking deeper meanings when done with noble intentions set to glorify our Messiah. But as for the oral tradition specific to the symbolism in this story (and the association to shepherding), I've embraced it. Again, you can discern judgement for yourself.

Realize this is not meant to be melodramatic, but the story does give a new perspective and draws focus into another way we can see our Master, the Good Shepherd. And in the *walk of walks*, it bears sharing as do all good things given by the Lord. Let's not withhold the graces that brings us hope and encouragement and helps cement our faith in Him and His ways.

So now, the question is this...

When you were young, did you ever rebel and try to run away...?

En Gedi Wilderness Reserve

Photo by J. Young

I have wandered away like a lost sheep;

come and find me,

for I have not forgotten Your commands.

Psalm 119:176 (NLT)

Chapter 7 - The Story

During the biblical times of the great sheepherders, there were days when the sheep weren't necessarily inclined to minding the directions of their masters. They too had problems with little one's wanting to go astray and have their own way. Intractable even. And to no surprise, whether it be sheep or children, nothing has changed over the centuries of time that has passed since. I guess that part of Darwin's evolutionary fallacy didn't progress as planned.

Regardless of generation, whether now or "way back then," as young ones, we usually hit some point in our life where we want to run and jump-the-fence (hence the question that closed the last chapter). We think the grass is greener on the other side, and life's purpose is to run free, unabated, unbanded, careless, and without restriction or restraint. It's an open road and the independence so longed for is just over there. Same now as it was then.

As the story is told…it was custom for the earliest shepherds of the field to cripple (even break) the leg of a lost little lamb if one continually decided to stray or bolt from the flock, thereby forcing the rebellious little-one to thereon be carried until it had healed, foiling the ability to run away anytime soon. This was thought to be not only an effective training tool, but also a manner of enforcing a type of re-bonding period. To give the best present-day reference, it was something commonly referred to as "tough-love." In sum, the "lost sheep" would become endeared to the shepherd by this crippling with the sole intention to repair the personal relationship while healing in the physical.

Now, during this process of intentionality, the lamb would no longer be able to have the freedom of choice or way. It would become totally and fully dependent upon the shepherd for everything. The shepherd would then be able to apply disciplined teaching through this onset of absolute dependency and renewal.

The shepherd would undertake a tasking of retraining the wounded little-one with instruction, discipline, patience, and love. In turn, the lost sheep would re-learn the voice of the shepherd, restoring the relationship and a newly developed desire to seek obedience and curry the shepherd's favor. This would result in giving them both time to become closely bonded again. Just like "Footprints in the Sand" ...

As followers of Jesus, we know we will have trials, tribulations, persecutions, troubled waters, and we will be held accountable to give that account of our life in response to such things (Matthew 5:10-12; 10:16; John 15:18-21; Romans 12:14; 14:12; 2 Corinthians 4:8-9; 5:10; Philippians 1:29-30; 2 Timothy 2:3; 1 Peter 4:12-16). Admittedly, some of us have wandered (even bolted) for sinful things guised as greener pastures. Yet it is in those times that the Lord waits patiently for us to hear the Spirit's grieving, turn around, and return to His sheepfold. His hands and arms are always waiting wide open, hoping for His little ones to return where they belong (Isaiah 44:22; Jeremiah 24:7; Joel 2:12-13; 1 Corinthians 16:23).

Again, I was taken because there was a personal familiarity with the story. In 2006, God "broke my leg" in the same fashion and manner (and intent) of those shepherds. I had risen to levels of prominence in terms of title, occupation, financial-gain, and prideful indifference. I needed exactly what the *Good, Good Father* ordered. I was bolting away, and He wasn't going to tolerate a single day more. I lost my job, my closest friends, and was left with no career pathway forward.

In sum, Jesus broke the yoke of my worldly desires and sinful lifestyle, hoping I would respond with a longing to return unto Him for forgiveness and restoration. He wanted everything back that I was crediting to myself so I could begin furthering His kingdom, not mine (Matthew 6:19-21). It was time to glorify Him fully and put an end to self-idolization and the sorrowful pride I had within myself. I needed to change my tune and raise a different banner of choice and way. The lifestyle I was living was only hastening a surefire path to self-destruction and a woeful demise.

Sounds so contrary to human understandings, but when finally realizing what had happened, I was overjoyed to be broken. Surely not at the moment, but with the gift of clear hindsight, it was exactly what was needed in order to return to His sheepfold. Yet most evident through it all, Jesus wanted me to hear His voice and learn to walk again. As David wrote in Psalm 51, "Make me to hear joy and gladness. Let the bones which You have broken rejoice."

So, I began to research **the story**…

Pools at En Gedi

Wild donkey near Monastery of Saint George
Jericho

Photos by J. Young

Help me, LORD my God;

Save me according to Your mercy. Let them know that it is

Your hand, that You, LORD, have done it.

Psalm 109:26~27

Chapter 8 - Let's Be Careful

Let me first say this – Do I believe that the shepherds of biblical times physically broke the legs of little lambs to prevent them from running away and thereby also allowing a time for them (the shepherds) to carry and nurture the lost one back to health? I leaned slightly hesitant, even chary. Sure, it could be plausible based on the intention and result, but we need to be cautious before we dive headlong. Could a shepherd have hurt or restricted one in his care when angry or fed-up with the constant chaos of a perceived, yet naïve, rebellion (i.e. "running away")? Absolutely. But this would seem to be a very rare exception, not necessarily a skilled example to be passed down through generations of shepherding craftsmen.

As a person who has had a lifetime of loving stewardship (and emergency assistance) over many types of animals, including dogs, cats, horses, mini-donkeys, hedgehogs, new born wild-bunnies, Houdini-goats, birds flying down chimneys into the house, butterflies with stuck wings, trapped baby deer, and a few aquarium fish, it is just too hard to consider hurting them for any reason. If you've ever had to "put down" a pet, you know the incredible amount of sorrow and pain that goes with it (and that's when it's in their best interest in sparring them from further suffering).

Responding in likeness to the cultural norms of the early 21st century, and being completely dependent upon the internet, I too decided to look the story up on the Google. Spoiler alert - I'll spare you the time. The most robust arguments from historians, theologians, and "the experts" themselves will tell you <u>no, the shepherds would not break the legs of any sheep in their care.</u>

The possibility (and subsequent running with the story) seems to stem from misinterpretations of the words "brake" verses "break" within their historical context and intent. Thus, the confusion was formed, giving birth to the misconception within the story. With the interchanging of meanings within the word usage, the story has a whole new meaning.

In 2006, a gentlemen named John O. (no relation) was on the same quest to determine if the legend was true. He too searched the internet and other sources for any information that would lend credibility to the story. After exhausting several other avenues of research, he decided to go directly to a different source of logical reliability - Sheep! magazine.

In the response to John's inquiry, the editor of Sheep!, Nathan Griffen wrote, "What they sometimes do in certain sheep-raising nations is to "brake" a leg. This means they attach a clog or weight to the animal's leg, which keeps certain "rogue" sheep from getting too far from the shepherd until they learn their names, and not to be afraid of the shepherd."[20]

Frankly, this made much more sense in terms of shepherding techniques. It also explains the mistaking of terms as "brake" and "break" are heard the same but clearly have a different word usage and meaning. Obviously, they are homonyms, which makes them easily mistakable when spoken and not written. You get the point. Word usage and understanding is essential in this regard.

Again, it might have been a stretch in believing that shepherds would truly break a leg of one in their care. But then again, I would have struggled with watching the sacrifices at the Tabernacles and Temples of the Old Testament. Realize, there were no chairs in the places of sacrifice because the priests never had time to sit down (Hebrews 10:11). There was so much bloodletting, no need for chairs. In this regard, it gave some plausibility to the shepherd's story, especially from the perspective of watching a Levite priest who was constantly sacrificing animals and meticulously sprinkling blood as required.

I do however believe that **when a small lamb got hurt or wounded during the normal course of things, the shepherd would surely carry them for means of necessity and their survival**. This is the essence of a shepherd's calling. The lamb would still need to go to-and-from the sheepfold for grazing, water, and for other needs. Doesn't seem likely the shepherds would leave a helpless lamb back in the fold without someone allocated to also staying behind.

In reflection, it's the opposite of leaving the flock of ninety-nine for the one that strays. Here the one left behind is not left alone, not by any means. So, whether it was daily routine or typical nomadic migrations, without doubt, the little lambs were carried when lame or needing help. Just like the picture…

Now in terms of the symbolism in the story – Absolutely…I get it! Has the Lord God allowed pain and suffering of His own? Just having a superficial understanding of the history of the Jewish people would answer that question (not intended to be examined or outlaid here). God allows suffering to help teach individuals and to provide a path of repentance or a clarified understanding essential to grow our faith (Deuteronomy 8:2-5; Psalm 119:67-76; John 9:1-3; Romans 8:28; 1 Peter 1:6-7; James 1:2-4; Hebrews 12:5-6, 10-11).

Born-again believers know this. It's what allows us to navigate those seasons of suffering and pain. Many times, it's simply to return the focus upon Him where it always belongs. Although it's hard to understand in this regard, heed the words of Paul in Romans 8:38-39 to comfort this hard truth:

For I am convinced that neither death nor life, neither angels nor demons, neither the present nor the future, nor any powers, neither height nor depth, nor anything else in all creation, will be able to separate us from the love of God that is in Christ Jesus our Lord.

One example of suffering beyond the Israelites of Exodus that must come to the mind of every believer is of course, the greatest story ever told

– Jesus, the Lamb of God.

For God so loved the world that He gave His only begotten Son, that whoever believes in Him should not perish but have everlasting life. For God did not send His Son into the world

to condemn the world, but that the world through Him might
be saved.

John 3:16-17 (NIV)

For the longest time, I struggled with trying to understand how God could be satisfied (even tolerant), with His Son being brutally beaten and flailed upon the Cross. Or how God could allow such sufferings of His created (both Jew and Gentile). Arguably, it is one of the most difficult things for Followers of Christ to understand. Yet through the eyes of sacrifice that granted our salvation, it becomes grace within the Passion. One passage that comes to mind is from the writings of Paul:

But God demonstrates his own love for us in this: While we
were still sinners, Christ died for us. Since we have now been
justified by his blood, how much more shall we be saved from
God's wrath through him! For if, while we were God's
enemies, we were reconciled to him through the death of his
Son, how much more, having been reconciled, shall we be
saved through his life!

Romans 5:8-10 (NIV)

The disciple whom Jesus loved reminds us:

This is how God showed His love among us: He sent His one and only Son into the world that we might live through Him. This is love: not that we loved God, but that He loved us and sent His Son as an atoning sacrifice for our sins.

1 John 4:9-10 (NIV)

Something beyond special is the way to see our relationship with Christ Jesus. It's uniquely crafted, intrinsically purposed, and intimately nurtured throughout our days numbered. Each moment is an opportunity for our genuine response to His intentions and His will for us. Again, it's how we respond that carries the weight of our deeds judged (Leviticus 26:3; Numbers 15:40; Deuteronomy 5:29; 11:13; 1 Kings 3:14; 9:4-7; 11:38; 2 Chronicles 7:17-20; Nehemiah 1:9; Proverbs 2:1-5; 7:1-2; Isaiah 48:18; John 14:15, 21; 15:10). Obey the Lord thy God, and all will be blessed before you (Exodus 12:24; 19:5; Leviticus 18:4-5; 25:18-19; 26:1-13; Deuteronomy 4:40; 5:29; 6:24-25; 11:1, 26-28; 12:28; 28:1-2; 30:1-10; Psalm 1:1-3; 19:8-11; Proverbs 3:1-2; Isaiah 1:19; Luke 11:28; John 14:15; James 1:25; 1 John 5:3; 2 John 1:6). It was that way in Eden, and it's that way today. Not even time has changed this absolute truth. And as you can see by the above references, it's overwhelmingly pure in its veracity and intent.

There are moments that seem to set that perfectly effective time to pause and be assured -You will never be abandoned, you will never be forsaken, you will never be lost, and you will never be snatched from His mighty hand (Deuteronomy 4:29-31; 1 Kings 6:13; Nehemiah 9:19; Psalm 9:10; 16:10; 37:25; John 10:28; 17:12)! Maybe just a simple reminder, but it's something so essentially valuable. Jesus knew you before you were woven (Psalm 139:13-16; Jeremiah 1:5). He knew exactly how He wanted to craft you, and He can't wait to see what you'll become (Psalm 138:13-14). And to think that some people thought He was only a meager Carpenter from that insignificant and paltry hillside village of Nazareth (John 1:46).

Jesus truly is our unfailing and ever-faithful Savior of love. The pictures of Jesus caring for the wounded lamb are meant to have countless meanings, symbolisms, and attachments in this regard. Explore and savor each one. Devote daily to Him and see what He unveils before you. Sometimes, the tapestry is just threads away from something you longed to know was always there. Be at peace and be still, know He is God (Psalm 37:7; 46:10). And He's coming:

Be still before the LORD,
all mankind, because He has roused Himself
from His holy dwelling.
Zechariah 2:13 (NIV)

The Garden Tomb – Jerusalem

The Galilee Shores, Israel

Photos by J. Young

Many are the plans in a person's heart,
but it is the LORD's purpose that prevails.
Proverbs 19:21 (NIV)

Chapter 9 ~ Can good really come from bad?

If you have ever come to some form of a "crossroads" in your life you will know that eventually a decision has-to be made. And those big-time choices come with some form of consequence. Something has-to be conceded in order to move forward. Something has-to be sacrificed. Turning back is just not possible because it's never really an option. It's just a façade of false hope. Think about it, otherwise you wouldn't be "staring down the fork" as they say. Something has-to give. Regardless of whether it's spiritual or physical in requirement, it is absolutely consequential in effect – as it should be. Choices must be made. Inaction may just be kicking the can down the road and delaying the inevitable. To quote a finely crafted lyrical favorite, "If you chose not to decide, you still have made a choice."[21] Spiritually, cue the agnostic, apathetic and the lukewarm (Revelation 3:16).

Can good things really result from bad things? Absolutely…just look at any reborn believer!

Like some, I have been the wounded lamb at the crossroads. From my wasted days of youth (pun intended), to the scariest of moments throughout, you can say I've woefully explored, surveyed and mapped "rock-bottom." I was running away from things I knew to be right because I didn't want to acknowledge the things I knew to be wrong. I was making my own ways, fixing my own footpaths. Arms folded in defiance and posturing in full rebellion. I was a donkey[22] with the ears pinned back, disciplined to my own tune. I knew Jesus was there, watching and waiting, but I hadn't had my leg broken, at least not yet. I needed a brake, just like the rebellious little lamb.

We can draw to the most basic of answers when we pose the question of good coming from bad. There are many who were exampled in the Scriptures that were lost sheep that the Lord broke or disciplined in-order to bring repentance and restoration. Some knew better and still gave-in to wrongdoing and sin. Although father of many nations, Abraham was a liar who profited greatly from it (Genesis 12:11-20). Jacob the same. He stole his brother's inheritance, and it nearly got him killed (Genesis 27:5-45).

We have the Egyptian-raised Moses who murdered (Exodus 2:11-12), then in direct disobedience to God struck the rock at Meribah (Numbers 20:7-13). Consequently, he only saw the Promised Land from afar after being denied entry because of his actions (Deuteronomy 32:51-52). Yet, Moses was one of our greatest prophets and biblical figures. Good from bad.

Consider further, David was a plotter, murderer, and adulterer, and it cost him his son (2 Samuel 11:1-12:19). He had quite the time during adolescence and then stumbled greatly at times as he aged. Although his heart was after God's, he was denied the honor of building the Temple (1 Chronicles 22:7-10). But, in the end, He was king of Israel and one of the greatest psalmists. Again, we see good coming from bad.

David was also father of the wisest man who ever lived (1 Kings 3:12; 4:29-31). Yet even Solomon fell and gave way to earthly fixations, especially with foreign women and idolatry at the leading of his wives (1 Kings 11:1-8). Although he was wise, he followed evil in the eyes of the Lord and would bear the consequences of God's judgement (1 Kings 11:6, 9, 11-13). But Solomon built the Temple and gave us some of the wisest writings of Scripture (Proverbs, Ecclesiastes, Song of Songs).

Hard to argue, Saul to Paul is of the greatest of reclamation projects recorded in the Scriptures (Acts 7:58-8:3; 9:1-31). He was a huge persecutor of Christians before his conversion. He willfully approved the stoning of Stephen (Acts 7:54-58; 8:3). Surely not the way to acknowledge such an incredible preaching witness and Stephen's compassionate forgiveness in the face of death (Acts 7:60). Yet, Paul was converted and subsequently authored a large portion of the New Testament, also becoming one of the greatest missionary church planters in history. He humbly reminds us, "Do not be overcome by evil, but overcome evil with good" (Romans 12:21).

There are so many examples, we won't truly know them all until later. But suffice it to say, we have enough to know the unstoppable power of forgiveness and restoration brought through the love of Christ. Jesus was, is, and shall always be, the pre-eminent (omni-eminent) example for us, perfected in all His glory.

If you are familiar with the 2005 documentary film called 'End of the Spear', you will quickly associate the truth of knowing evil can be overcome by good. Based on actual events in 1956, Operation Auca was the attempt of American Christian missionaries to evangelize the Waodani people in the tropical rain forest of Eastern Ecuador. During the undertaking, five male missionaries were speared to death by a group of the Waodani tribe and their maddened leader.

The movie is told from the perspective of Steve Saint (son of Nate Saint, one of the missionaries killed in the encounter), and Mincaye, a tribesman leader who participated in the attack. Based on resilience, love, and compassion, Mincaye was later convicted of his actions, even forging a lifelong relationship with Steve. It's an amazing story of persistence, faith, and hope.

Good can overcome evil, we just need to never give up, never give in, and never forget. These are the infallible character qualities folded within a resilient and unbounded faith.

Finally, just look in the mirror. If you have asked Jesus for forgiveness of all your sins and for Him to be your Savior, you're something that was bad, but now good. Much like filthy rages, you've been washed anew (Isaiah 64:6). Everyone celebrates when a sinner repents and seeks forgiveness (Luke 15:7, 10)! Truly, any human who has been born-again and has given their life to following Christ Jesus is a lost sheep who has been found. So really, good comes from bad all the time. But it must be fused with intention and love, just as He taught us. In the scope of salvation's fullness, it takes two. Christ Jesus fulfilled His part, always serving the will of the Father (John 5:19; 6:38-39; 8:28). Let's help others reach to fulfill theirs.

The completeness in concept of the Good Shepherd and the lost sheep is fully revealed in Luke chapter 15 – The Parable of the Lost Sheep. This model of shepherding is so important that the Holy Spirit dedicated this passage for such intentionality. It tends to be a go-to for the most enthusiastic evangelist because it outlays such a compassionate approach to restoration and the need to see things through the lenses of love and forgiveness.

The Lord is beyond our full understanding, and we know His ways are not our ways. Uniquely, this intention allows us to propagate roots of faith that strengthens our desire to serve Him and seek others (Matthew 16:24-27, Luke 17:5-6). We need to long for the voice of our Shepherd so we can grow to be good and faithful servants straightaway and without delay (Matthew 10:38; 16:24; John 10:27; 1 Peter 4:19). Yes, we want to hear those words later as we give our account, but let's live it in the here-and-now. Let's bring forth fruit that bears a lifestyle evangelism that draws others to seek Him without a second thought.

It is true, the grass can be greener on the other side, but realize our Good Shepherd is watching from higher pastures. He wants to see how His sheep will carry-on in His perceived absence and without the cognizant realization He is observing everything.

It is the opposite of what is called the Hawthorne Effect. Here, individuals reactively modify aspects of their behavior in response to their awareness of being observed.[23] As Believers, we need to be living in a lifestyle that is a natural state of righteousness as our norm, not the exception (as if someone is watching from outside the fence).

Do we know Jesus is ever-present and always watching over us? Of course we do. But can we walk in daily righteousness without a reactive posturing or concern over our image (i.e. the public perception)? That's the real question. It's ironic that many Christians tend to worry more about what others feel about them personally as opposed to what we know will not be hidden from His sight (Hebrews 4:13).

To worry more about other's perceptions instead of the desires of the Lord's is woefully human, but so backwards in priority and need. I too have fallen prey to such failings. It's an easy trap because most people want to be liked, regardless. It's human nature to seek favor, popularity, and fame, but the Lord sees everything, knows everything, and considers it all.

David reminds us of this in Psalm 139:

You have searched me, LORD, and You know me. You know when I sit and when I rise; You perceive my thoughts from afar. You discern my going out and my lying down; You are familiar with all my ways. Before a word is on my tongue You, LORD, know it completely. You hem me in behind and before, and You lay Your hand upon me. Such knowledge is too wonderful for me, too lofty for me to attain. Where can I go from Your Spirit? Where can I flee from Your presence? If I go up to the heavens, You are there; if I make my bed in the depths, You are there. If I rise on the wings of the dawn, if I settle on the far side of the sea, even there Your hand will guide me, Your right hand will hold me fast. If I say, "Surely the darkness will hide me and the light become night around me," even the darkness will not be dark to You; the night will shine like the day, for darkness is as light to You. For You created my inmost being; You knit me together in my mother's womb. I praise You because I am fearfully and wonderfully made; Your works are wonderful, I know that full well. My frame was not hidden from You when I was made in the secret place, when I was woven together in the depths of the earth. Your eyes saw my unformed body; all the days ordained for me were written in Your book before one of them came to be.

Psalm 139:1-16 (NIV)

In the societal norms of social media and such, Jesus is the only One you should be concerned with "liking" your post. While others are nice, His is the one most worthy. Would you rather have 1.6K likes of some worthless rambling seeking worldly approval, or one favored by the Lord Jesus Christ, stamped with His "Like" 👍 ???

Yah, me too!

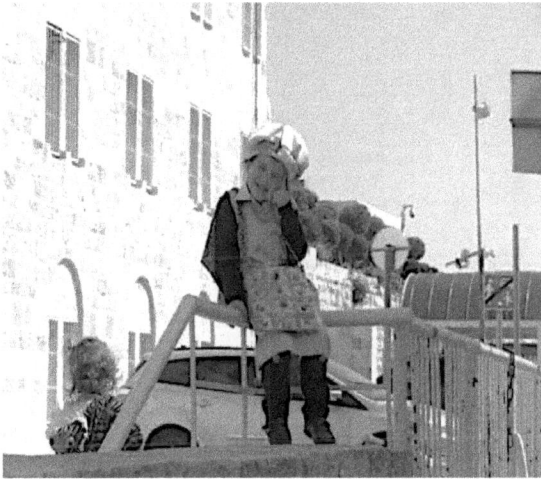

A young Jewish boy celebrating Purim[24] - Jerusalem

Photo by J. Young

I know the LORD is always with me.

I will not be shaken, for He is right beside me.

Psalm 16:8 (NLT)

Chapter 10 ~ Cry out to Jesus...I

Have you ever felt so depressed, so defeated, so lost and hurt that you couldn't speak or move? Times where the weight of things were so heavy that breathing became constrictive, even desperate? It's like having the wind knocked out of you. Those familiar with this know it as a form of anxiety. And in its heightened levels, it's absolutely terrifying because the ability to inhale or exhale just isn't there. Unfortunately, many of us have experienced this and it's something we wouldn't ever want to go through again. In such times, depression and/or anxiety can be dangerous because there is a darkened spiritual gravity that Satan wields with much mastery, much in the way of a full-seizing through a mental-type bondage.

In commentary of Psalm 88, the great theologian Charles Spurgeon wrote, "The mind can descend far lower than the body, for in it there are bottomless pits. The flesh can bear only a certain number of wounds and no more, but the soul can bleed in ten thousand ways, and die over and over again each hour."[25]

The reality is that it's a fallen world, roamed and ravaged by the fallen one – Satan. He's powerful, but not All-Powerful. He's cunning, but not All-Knowing. He does wander to-and-fro throughout the earth (Job 1:7), but he is not Ever-Present. He is created, not the Creator. Although his ambitions were to be equal, he became the father of all lies – a murder from the beginning (John 8:44). A fallen-angel temporarily allowed to rule a fallen world (Isaiah 14:13-14, 1 John 5:19). He's only biding time, leaving unreserved destruction through a wake of evil intent and a ruin of aftermath. But again, he's just biding his time. May we lift the prayer of the saints as recorded in Revelation, chapter 6:

And they cried out with a loud voice, saying, "How long, O Lord, holy and true, will You refrain from judging and avenging our blood on those who dwell on the earth?"

Revelation 6:10

We know we will be tested, burdened, tempted, trialed, and persecuted (James 1:2). Remember though, this is a double blessing when we face such times (Matthew 5:10-11). We are blessed by understanding it is Him we need to call upon (Psalm 18:3). It doesn't matter whether we break our own leg via our own missteps, or He brakes it for us, it's the response that matters.

The author of Hebrews reminds us why some of us need to be broken. He tells us, "Endure hardship as discipline; God is treating you as His children. For what children are not disciplined by their father?" (Hebrews 12:7). So, do we drag ourselves along, relying on our own crutches of pride and postering, or do we seek the only One who can reset our life and reilluminate the true footpath of righteousness (Proverbs 12:28). Make no mistake, the first step is to cry out to Jesus.

If we make our own decisions at the crossroads of life instead of leaning upon Jesus (Proverbs 3:5-6), we allow our desires and appeals to influence us away from righteous wisdom. Many times, we do not make the right decisions because it is far harder than the perceived easier path. We give way to emotions by turning away from realities. We rationalize decisions via our own human understanding until it overcomes our spiritual convictions. Bad step.

Sadly, when we fall prey to such problematic conditions, we get more comfortable suffocating the Spirit than seeking His divine wisdom (Ephesians 4:30). We think we're going forward when we're actually losing ground on the sandhill of trials and tribulations. It's like walking on an escalator the wrong way. Might be fun as a kid, but as we get older it becomes grueling, tiresome, even futile. Older yet, becomes something we cannot overcome without major assistance. But then again, why do things that are fruitlessly exhausting and have no heavenly value?

How we respond to hardship, failures, or losses, can either agitate and impair the situation or it can glorify the Lord with examples of humility, forgiveness, grace, mercy, servitude, sacrifice, and love. Easier said than done, especially in the moment, but therein is the opportunity if you can step back and rely upon the Lord to lead you through those dark valleys wherein only He can abate such fears. Yea though I walk…(Psalm 23).

Not only is crying out to Jesus a good first step, it's also one that gets us back on His blessed footpath. No matter if you've been walking with Him for decades, or rebelling the same, you have to start here if you're going to start again. You must pivot the right direction and take a step of intentionality. Maybe it's just the need to turn-around.

It is important to know that if you feel convicted, it's ok to jump right into His arms. Much like stopping, dropping, and praying for something in an immediate moment of need. Sometimes the trials of life are simple embers just lying in wait for a titch of wind to provoke them into a fire that soon gets out of control.

It draws me to a much beloved safety warning that many generations of children grew up with when we were taught fire safety in public schools and such. If your clothing caught fire, we were taught by our local firemen to "Stop-Drop-and-Roll." Here, the spiritual need is no different - Stop, drop and pray!

If you've ever watched a movie with people who are stranded and trying to survive as they are caught in a life-threatening situation, they sometimes rely on emergency flares to help draw attention to their dooming situation. A small handheld gun would shoot a flare that emits a trailing tail of sparkling fireworks that explode into a bright light high in the air. This would then notify anyone close of their location and that they needed help. Whether marooned on a remote island or lost at sea while drifting in a makeshift lifeboat, an emergency flare can be the last hope to being saved. And in truth, they have saved many people in the direst of situations.

Prayers can be the same in cause and effect. You may even hear Believers refer to these emergency pleas for help as "flare prayers" because we find ourselves in precarious or dangerous situations where hope seems to be running out and we feel left to our last resorts. Or there may be a severe and immediate need and we're compelled to act without haste. Either way, we throw-up a flare prayer…like a desperate and lost little lamb crying out to be found.

We need to be careful though to not see the Lord as a last resort by forgoing all prayer and petition prior to landing in such challenging circumstances. All too often, people refuse to turn to Jesus until the last minute or until they feel their life is in jeopardy. As an example, although "death bed" confessions and conversions are common, it forgoes all the opportunities a person had to a life serving Jesus Christ prior to their last moments. Such wasted time in such regard. It may also diminish a person's account with Christ to only mere moments of joy when people wait till the last mortal moment to seek Him for salvation.

Yes, there is rejoicing that a person finally came to Christ, but again, what about all the time lost prior? Will Jesus ask, "My child, what about all those days and blessings I gave you and you simply stayed afar?" It's disheartening thinking that this may be a question that might be facing those who defer till the last moment. Here, my question is why wait? Why does anyone wait?

One of the great gifted skillsets in people we call "prayer warriors" is their determined discipline (and obedience) within the effectiveness of preemptive prayer. They know that prayer without ceasing is proactive and shows intention to staying alert and being ever-ready for life's twists and turns (Romans 12:12; 1 Thessalonians 5:17). And not only for themselves, more-so for others (Romans 12:13-18). It also affirms an obedient mindset to be observant of evangelistic opportunities at each day's onset. My mom is a great prayer warrior. She and a group of similar like-hearted friends pray together every breaking morning. They are my spiritual heroines.

But again, if you feel caught in what seems like a hopeless situation, seek the Lord's urgent help and mercy. Call for a quick-carry assist. Seek divine aid from the only One who can bring us back to restoration and life. His path is always best.

It's odd, but sometimes people ask why they can't hear God? They wonder how others seem to have such clarity with God, while they themselves struggle with the sounds of silence. Not always the case, but many times it's as simple as recognizing one's posture towards God, or lack thereof.

Imagine trying to instruct a very young child. They generally start by facing you and giving you some form of attention. But as they grow, they eventually start to adjust their position based on their own personal feelings of understanding, experience, and a gradually diminishing attention span. Soon, they turn away with their back against you as your trying to speak to them. Already we have a position of defiance and rebellion. When allowed, this pattern then strengthens, and the child starts to walk away…step by step, until they're running without knowing. You keep talking, even yelling, trying to bring them back to solid footing, but after too long, they're too far away to hear even the loudest of pleas to stop running.

Here, a person must turn around. Turn back and see the arms of the Shepherd wide open and know He's willing to carry you if you just come back to Him. The turn and return allows a lost one to start seeing and hearing the voice of redemption and healing. People either turn around and face it or they stand in defiance against it. But nothing will change until the posture is corrected.

Turning and facing God is a step that cannot be skipped. You can't see Him if your back is against Him, (let alone the posture it signals). And you can't hear Him if your hands are covering your ears. Forget staying in your own lane and get back into His. No path is straighter, and no way is more righteous. Forgiveness of sin and the promise of eternal salvation comes through one way. We surely are not the first ones to need a navigational correction in this regard.

Don't worry, Thomas got clarification…

Thomas said to Him, "Lord, we don't know where You are going, so how can we know the way?" Jesus answered, "I am the way and the truth and the life. No one comes to the Father except through Me.

John 14:5-6 (NIV)

Steps at Banias Falls – Hermon Stream Nature Reserve

Photo by J. Young

Let me hear Your lovingkindness in the morning;

For I trust in You; Teach me the way in which I should walk;

For to You I lift up my soul.

Psalms 148:8

Chapter 11 - It's Much Easier to Walk
Than to Be Carried

As my dad used to say, "That sounds cattywampus." This happens to be a slang term for something that is askew, not right, or something that's totally off. By human understandings, it would seem obvious that it takes far less energy to have someone carry you as opposed to walking yourself. Agreed.

Even as kids, to be lifted onto someone's shoulders or on their back turned out to be an awesome form of conveyance. No question, having an overzealous grandpa or someone else that could give you a camelback-ride was a good deal. But as we got older, you realize being carried somehow means you lose freedoms. Hard not to notice the screaming kid at the store who wants to be let down out of the cart so they can run around and touch everything! You get the picture.

Spiritually, going from being carried to walking is like the phrase *getting your legs under you*. Often this is said to encourage people to get up after they've been knocked down. More so to motivate them to start picking themselves up and start moving again. Whether it's an exhausted mountain climber on the decent from Mt. Everest wanting to give-in or a fighter who just got leveled to the canvas floor, you've got to get up and start moving if you want to help your situation.

When spiritually broken, abilities to self-motivate into corrective action often seems impossible at the time, especially at the onset of what's happened. We feel the immediate impact of what's gripping our brokenness and it throws us into tailspins in what to do next. Many people have shared their experiences of feeling utterly lost and without any breadcrumb of hope or direction. Feeling seized and defeated, people often overlook the pathway out.

Whether we ourselves are feeling overpowered and overwhelmed, or we're watching a loved one going through something equally painful, encouragement to see hope again is a critical action. In such circumstances, we need to draw-in and remember we have hope. Next to love, hope is a powerful motivator to get up and face the challenge (1 Corinthians 13:13). When hope and love are forged together...nearly impossible to fail.

Not making light of this (or trying to state the obvious), but **our Good Shepherd is exactly as advertised! He is righteousness within righteousness, that surrounds righteousness, fulfilling, perfecting, and completing all righteousness.** He's the Shepherd that carries His wounded and heals the lame. He's everything we hope Him to be, even though we may struggle at times to see it that way. Far too often, people blame God when the roads get rough or clouded with life's wicked turns. Especially when those seasons are filled with tragedy or death. Again, such a human failing to be so shortsighted and impugning of God's sovereignty and love for us. We just fail to see it at times. Truly, it's better to be blinded to this world in order to see His kingdom and purpose more clearly.

It shouldn't be surprising we have such difficulties handling things like death. Aside the devastating effects of emotional loss and deep emptiness, we experience metal anguish and sufferings that often place us in the lowest point of human conditions. Realize though, we were not fashioned to deal with death. God created us in His image, and that image wasn't purposed for sin, evil, or death (Genesis 1:26). When officiating at funerals or within the scope of counseling, reminding others of this helps navigate the overwhelming gamut of emotions tied to dealing with the loss of a loved one, especially the feelings of losing direction and hope. It's so difficult because it wasn't part of our original purpose or crafting.

We simply weren't meant to deal with death and the passing of those we love and care for. It wasn't part of the original design. However, due to our sin and transgressions, now we must. There is no good textbook way to really handle death, but the biblical way is to be comforted by the Lord because true comfort can only come from Him (Matthew 5:4). That's why He gives us this teaching. We're not blessed because we mourn the death of someone, it's because if we seek Him when we mourn, He will comfort us. Therein is the blessing and the real meaning behind the picture of Jesus carrying His hurt and wounded. He's there when we need Him the most, and utmost.

People often quip, "Time heals all wounds." I see this is as another fallacy of life. Time does not heal wounds. Only the comfort of Jesus does that. Time simply allows us to navigate it easier because we eventually get used to the loss and the absence. We surrender to the realities and accept there is nothing more that can be done. Scars eventually cover the wounds and we try to move forward. The scars remain (and remind), so we simply find ways to press on. There really isn't much of a choice. Time keeps moving whether we like it or not.

Mercifully, provision has been made, and death has been subjected unto Him (1 Corinthians 15:27). God revealed the path of dealing with sin back when Adam and Eve's eyes were *opened* and they made the veil attempt to cover their own sin (Genesis 3:7). Leaves of fig trees were just a frail attempt at satisfying a requirement they couldn't do on their own. God killed the first animal, blood was shed, and skins were provided to cover their sin and shame (Genesis 3:21).

That was the foreshadowing for things to know and understand as mankind moved forward. Hereon, blood and sacrifices unending. But that was only until Jesus came. The requirement for sin's penalty has not been abated by any means. Blood must be shed for the wages of sin is death (Romans 6:23). But as we know, Jesus paid the penalty for those who believe. John the Baptist saw it and knew it firsthand:

Behold, the Lamb of God who takes away the sin of the world!
John 1:29

Though death was brought by sin, God has granted forgiveness through His Son. His willing sacrifice to pay those wages granted us the provision for forgiveness and eternal life. The profit Isaiah reminds us, "He will swallow up death for all time, And the Lord GOD will wipe tears away from all faces, And He will remove the reproach of His people from all the earth; For the LORD has spoken" (Isaiah 25:8). We now echo the sentiments of Paul saying, "O DEATH, WHERE IS YOUR VICTORY? O DEATH, WHERE IS YOUR STING?" (1 Corinthians 15:55).

Yes, Jesus wants to be there to take our burdens and pain, but I believe He desires that to be when we're unable or unequipped to handle them spiritually ourselves. He wants to help us walk so we can learn to run. Believe it or not, we do have a race before us (1 Corinthians 9:24-27; Philippians 2:16; 3:14). And as the author of Hebrews reminds us:

Therefore, since we are surrounded by such a huge crowd of witnesses to the life of faith, let us strip off every weight that slows us down, especially the sin that so easily trips us up. And let us run with endurance the race God has set before us.
Hebrews 12:1

Let's put things into perspective. In which of these do you think Jesus places His hopes? That God's children will remain children in wisdom and stature, needing to be nursed on milk again (1 Corinthians 3:1-3; Philippians 2:15; Hebrews 5:13-14), or that we grow to display a lifestyle evangelism in love; one in that the world will know we are the children of God

(John 13:34-35)? Maybe it's time to understand our spiritual wounds more biblically and acknowledge the reality in their attempt to disrupt our relationship with Christ. If the flag is down, encourage your brother or sister to pick it up and start marching again. Again, hope and encouragement are powerful motivators when brought together with righteous intent.

We are to learn, through love, the teachings of Jesus. We are then to run a race worthy of His faith in us. We know our faith is core to our relationship with Him, but what about His faith in us in return? Many of the challenges He places in front of us are set to answer that very question. Wouldn't it be nice to hear "I knew you could do it – I had faith in you" before we hear the precious words, "Well done my good and faithful servant" (Matthew 25:21-23)?

His faith in us should be answered like the resilient and brave efforts that so many of our missionaries, evangelists, first-responders, military service personnel, and others similar have example every day. We know there is no greater love than to lay one's life down for another (John 15:13). Those who serve in such roles are willing to give such a gift, loving others as they would love themselves (Matthew 22:39). Can you imagine if all believers put forth such efforts to further the gospel? It might just hasten the Return.

Olives being harvested from the ancient trees in the Garden of Gethsemane

Photo by J. Young

My prayer is not that you take them out of the world but

that you protect them from the evil one.

John 17:15 (NIV)

Chapter 12 – Been there, done that…

I too was a lost sheep. Like so many, I found myself spinning outside of spiritual protections and their providence, and profiteering in the things of this world. Too many times I was jumping the spiritual guardrails so I could taste those supposedly *greener pastures* on the other side. Exploitations in wealth and excess were searingly addictive, and I eagerly embraced the illusionary prospering. Much like a passage in the

Old Testament that describes a condition of living in excess yet also failing to realize the grips of seductive appeals. Prosperity has a cunning way in its deceptions of success and opulence if not meant in its aims of glorifying God.

Remember the time in Egypt where Scripture records that Israel *planted their stakes* in Goshen, thriving in the prosperity of the land and growing in population?

Now the Israelites settled in Egypt in the region of Goshen. They acquired property there and were fruitful and increased greatly in number.

Genesis 47:27

According to Scripture, everything for the Israelites seemed good based on results of their settling. Without question, they grew in great size and gained much of the land. In essence, they were becoming a great nation as God declared they would. But what's failed in recognition is that this appearance of growth and success was also a precursor of affliction and bondage. They were becoming blind even though they could see.

The Hebrew translation for "and they acquired property" is the word 'āḥaz. This means "to be caught" or "to be held."[26] Drawn from a teaching taken from the great Rabbi Shlomo Yitzchaki [Rashi], "The word vayei'achazu ("they took

128

possession of it") literally means "they took hold of it," but also translates as "they were held by it." Rashi interprets vayei'achazu as related to the word achuzah meaning, "landholding" and "homestead"; the Midrash[27] interprets it to imply that "the land held them and grasped them . . . like a man who is forcefully held."[28]

So, while the impression is that they (the Israelites) were doing great and being blessed while in Goshen...they were actually being held captive by the grips of their supposed prosperities. It's a curse and a blessing in a duel dependance. Rashi continues, "This duality defines the Jew's attitude toward *galut* (exile). On the one hand, we know that no matter how hospitable our host country may be, and no matter how we may flourish materially and spiritually on foreign soil, *galut* is a prison in that it dims our spiritual vision, hinders our national mission and compromises our connection with G-d."[29] Yes, Joseph was a front row witness for the way God was fulfilling the Abrahamic Covenant (Genesis 12:1-3; 13:5; 15:18-21), but the land purposed and promised was not Goshen, it was Canaan. The land of their host Egypt was holding them. It's reminiscent of someone who enjoys being in an unlocked jail because they don't know better of their condition. The door's open, but comfort of the known seems better than the freedom in the unknown. In sum, it's voluntary incarceration.

The land the Israelites were acquiring and using as a measure of their success was rising to grip and bond them. Again, it was a veiled captivity and became the precursor to Pharoh's bondage (Exodus 1:8-14). In the end, it was one of many consequences of their choices and indifferences. They weren't supposed to settle in permanency, rather to sojourn until the end of the famine. What was supposed to be 7-years removed, turned into nearly *seventy times seven*.

I too was living similar in apathy and context to the spiritual conditions as the Israelites. I was enjoying excessive living and a careless lifestyle. It was absent of spiritual discipline and filled with the embracing of things in this world. I was successful by the measures of men but grieving the Spirit without pause.

In cultural comparisons, I was comfortable spending time in Vegas and felt little remorse in being surrounded by sin. Ashamed now, but I probably wouldn't have raised issues then with the first-century Romans lavishing at Casearia Phillippi and admiring the Gates of Hell. Within me now, it raises a disgust and immediate repentance within the spirit and fervor of Elijah! I'm ashamed of who I was back then, but I've fully learned from it. Again, it's the response that matters.

Arguably, it's not that we've sinned that necessarily concerns God the most, it's how we respond (i.e. rebellion and denial or admittance and repentance). It's stunning to look back and see how comfortable I became with sin. Not the first person for sure, but it humiliates me now. I shudder when thinking of some of those darkened days of excess and indifference. Unfortunately, I know I'll be revisiting them when giving an account to Christ. This is a future experience I am ashamed to know is in front of me. Forgiveness has been given and is never in doubt, but it's all coming out and it will all be examined again directly with Christ (John 5:22; Romans 14:10-12; 2 Corinthians 5:10).

It is also something to heed carefully as you measure your daily deeds and actions (James 3:13). You do not want that accounting to be longer than it must. Eliminate the sin and repent, shorten that part of your account, and start pushing the walls of the kingdom outward to make room for more who are lost. Not lessoning its true impact, but it will be a much more comfortable conversation if you heed such wisdom without haste.

Fortunately, God's love for us is unfailing, rich in long-suffering (Psalm 6:4; 13:5; 21:7; 26:3; 31:16; 32:10; 33:5, 18; 2 Peter 3:9). At the height of my sinful and excessive lifestyle, He knew I needed to be broken. He also knew I need to be carried back to a right relationship with Him if we were ever going spent eternity together. I needed to relearn and long-for the Voice of the Good Shepherd. He didn't give up on me like I did with others. He broke my leg. Again, the question was…How would I respond?

As you know now, I decided I wanted to serve Him fully throughout my newly days numbered. I answered His calling and now deeply desire to only serve Him. No longer do I desire to serve myself or those temporary kingdoms and tissue-paper castles. I am a bondservant of Christ here, now, and forever more.

The question is, what's your status?

Caesarea Philippi – Northern Israel

Gates of Hell - Caesarea Philippi (Matthew 16:18)

Photos by J. Young

Even to your old age I will be the same,

And even to your graying years I will bear you!

I have done it, and I will carry you;

And I will bear you and I will deliver you.

Isaiah 46:4

Chapter 13 – Ok, now you got this...

Jesus will carry us when needed, but it is much better if we grow to walk alongside faithfully so He can have His hands to carry someone else. Can He carry us all? Of course He can. But the point is we need to be strong enough to bear our own cross in our desires to follow Him (Luke 14:27). Two distinct concepts but inclusive in nature and effect.

Let's call it what it is. Believe it or not, **all attacks are spiritual attacks** (Ephesians 6:12). Difference being, believers have been impowered to persevere through grace, mercy, and hope (Psalm 25:21, 33:18-22, 62:5, 119:114; 1 Corinthians 4;12; 10:13; Hebrews 10:36). We have the indwelling of the Holy Spirit, and we can seek the Lord's help to rebuke Satan (Jude 1:9-10). True believers are not blinded. We know Satan is very powerful and fully engaged in prowling this world in the most daunting and unnoticeable ways.

We know that we are children of God and that the world around us is under the control of the evil one.
   1 John 5:19 (NLT)

Christ provides us the armor to help us carry the fight against sin and withstand the attacks of evil (Ephesians 6:10-17). How do we know this? Well, did you notice that the Armor of God only has one offensive weapon and the rest is left for defenses? - "The Sword of the Spirit, which is the word of God." So not only are we righteously equipped with the best protections, but we are also given the ultimate weapon to defeat the attacks. Our Shepherd has not left us exposed or ill-prepared. Jesus has given us everything we need to carry a successful battle to completion. Not meant to be easy, but we are assured of victory with His hand.

But again ~ let's be careful! We are looking to defend and defeat the attack, not necessarily the attacker. Now that may sound odd, but even Michael the Archangel handled his encounter with Satan with much caution and discretion (Jude 1:9). He yielded the situation to Jesus. The defeat of Satan is certain, but it is at the province of the Lord (Revelation 20:10).

Only Christ has such power and authority to deal with the fate of the Fallen One. It's not semantics. Know the true object of the battle. We need to continue the fight against the temptations of sin and leave the ultimate fate of Satan to the Lord Jesus Christ. The Apostle Peter writes:

Be sober, be vigilant; because your adversary the devil walks about like a roaring lion, seeking whom he may devour. Resist him, firm in your faith, knowing that the same kinds of suffering are being experienced by your brotherhood throughout the world. ~ 1 Peter 5:8~9 (NKJV)

We cannot defeat Satan himself, but we can defeat everything he can possibly throw at us. His weapons are the lust and evil desires of mankind's heart. And those object desires are the lightning~rods to sin. We give it birth through temptation and the darkened fire is lit (James 1:15). Often, it's so quick it becomes unnoticed and therefore discounted, much of which is the exact intent of Satan. This pattern can easily lead

137

to an unhealthy tolerance and eventual indifference, if not ignorance (a tune many of us were familiar with until we turned around and sought refuge through forgiveness and restoration).

Consider, God came to Adam and Eve fully knowing they had violated the command not to eat of the fruit from the tree of knowledge of good and evil. And yet, He still allowed them the chance to come clean and be truthful (Genesis 3:9-11). Their response? They both pointed fingers at someone else, setting a woefully human pattern of avoidance and deferred accountability. Their firstborn son soon followed.

We credit the first sin to Adam for many reasons. When you slow the Scriptures down and devote discerning eyes to key details, you'll find even more of God's desire for you to know who He is. The command to not eat of the fruit from the tree in the midst of the Garden was given to Adam alone (Genesis 2:15-17). It was Adam's obligation to make sure this command was taught fully to Eve and understood clearly by her. He was the steward of truth and obedience for Eve and all who would follow.

Whether failing that responsibility or not, Adam didn't restrain Eve when taking the fruit. He was with her...

When the woman saw that the fruit of the tree was good for food and pleasing to the eye, and also desirable for gaining wisdom, she took some and ate it. She also gave some to her husband, who was with her, and he ate it.

Genesis 3:6 (NIV)

He allowed her to be tempted within a vulnerability that was his responsibility to oversee and protect. Satan simply exploited the opportunity as he always does. Beyond the fact Eve did not get the original command directly from God (again, it was only given to Adam), biblical commentator David Guzik notes three additional points in this regard:

- *Perhaps Satan knew by observation Adam didn't do an effective job of communicating to Eve what the LORD told him. This failure on Adam's part made Eve more vulnerable.*

- *Satan will often attack a chain at its weakest link, so he gets at Adam by tempting Eve. The stronger ones in a "chain" must expect an attack against weaker links and support them against those attacks.*

- *If Adam would have sinned first, and if he had then given the fruit to Eve, she might have a partial excuse before God: "I was simply obeying the head of our home. When he gave me the fruit, I ate of it."[30]*

Without fail, Satan surely calculated all this in his initial attack upon mankind. It's easy for us now to evaluate and clearly see these failings which allowed sin to prevail. God wanted us to know these vulnerabilities and the consequences of our disobedience if we acquiesce and give in. He wanted us to have clear eyes and a sober mind to live within the blessings of life. We are to learn from errors of those before us, even as early as Adam and Eve's.

We must be proactive in our defense against sin and yield the direct dealings of Satan up to the Son of Man to whom all authority has been given (Matthew 28:18). We need to master sin not Satan. Remember how God instructed Cain in his rebuke? Anger was the catalyst [the lightning rod] to his sin:

Then the LORD said to Cain, "Why are you angry? And why has your countenance fallen? If you do well, will not your countenance be lifted up? And if you do not do well, sin is crouching at the door; and its desire is for you, but you must master it.

Genesis 4:6~7

Even though God came to Cain fully knowing he was feeling rejected, downcast, even heated, He still allowed Cain the chance to heed cautionary wisdom and gain the upper hand on his sin. Cain could have told the truth and sought

140

forgiveness. He had the same chance as his Ima and Abba[31]. Yet he was already caught in the emotional grips of anger, jealousy, and a rage just waiting to be detonated! The result was the first murder in human history. Cain killed his brother Abel (Genesis 4:8).

Adam had a chance to be truthful (Genesis 3:11~12). Eve had a chance to be truthful (Genesis 3:13). Cain had a chance to be truthful (Genesis 4:9). I've often wondered what it would be like if Adam had only accepted responsibility for the original sin instead of blaming it on the woman God had given him. Would Eve have followed his example and confessed that she gave in to temptation? Would Cain have learned to control his jealousies and embrace being a keeper of his brother? Would Abel have lived another day as the first shepherd and keeper of the flock?

What would have happened had things been different in the original sin is irrelevant now. But is it curious to wonder how God's compassion would have unfolded had mankind responded with honesty and truth instead of lying. Would the patterns and precedents of lies and diversions in blaming others be replaced with genuine repentance as the natural action? It's a question every parent wonders when navigating those confrontations with their child(ren). More often than not, we know the truth of the situation, so our concern is more focused on a truthful confession and a hopeful ensuing regret because they did something wrong, not because they got caught and now face consequences. We want them to feel the moral convictions at the earliest of ages and develop strong attributes for truth and confronting sin.

Therefore, please know first and foremost ~ Don't disobey. Yes, it's that clear. May not be easy, but it's clear. Secondly, if we sin, don't dance around it and point the finger at someone else. God allowed mercy in asking Adam, Eve, and even Cain, what they had done before any consequence was given. And again, He fully knew what they did. God allowed them the chance to be forthright with their actions and claim responsibility. He simply asked. And He didn't yell.

It's also a good pattern for parents to example…give children a chance to tell the truth, even if you know what happened. Many positive things can come from affirmations of doing good (telling the truth) when children are struggling with decision making and peer pressure situations. Sometimes, just a little pinch of understanding and association can raze the walls built between children and their parents. It also expands our abilities to grow within patience and long suffering.

In our desires to walk worthy and righteous, the expertise and proficiency to thwarting sin and gaining the upper-hand has already been laid out. Do what is right, and you will be accepted; learn to rule over sin (Genesis 4:7). God wouldn't have said if it we didn't have the ability to do it.

Jerusalem, Israel

The Golden Gate – The Gate Beautiful
Jerusalem, Israel

Photos by J. Young

But He turned and said to Peter, "Get behind Me, Satan!
You are a stumbling block to Me; for you are not setting
your mind on God's interests, but man's.

Matthew 16:23

Chapter 14 - Get Behind me Satan!

For nonbelievers to think the attacks of life are not spiritually driven, well that's playing right into the Devil's hands. If they (nonbelievers) don't believe there are spiritual battles being fought, then they don't believe in Satan. Satan is a fallen angel of the spiritual world. The Apostle Paul affirms, "For our struggle is not against flesh and blood, but against the rulers, against the powers, against the world forces of this darkness, against the spiritual forces of wickedness in the heavenly places (Ephesians 6:12). Thus, if people don't believe in Satan, they'll have no reason to turn to God. Mission accomplished as far as Satan is concerned.

Satan just wants to keep the created from the Creator. It is taking children from their family – God's family (John 1:12; Romans 8:14; Galatians 3:26; Philippians 2:15; 1 John 3:9-10). Satan isn't seeking followers - he's seeking evil rebels. He wants the worldly rich and ruthless. He wants those who live self-exalted; those who's earthly works are written in history, yet sadly, have no name scribed in heaven (Luke 10:18-20).

As followers of Christ, when we get attacked, we need to know (1) how to recognize it, (2) how to treat it, and (3) how to respond to it. Each phase having its own unique set of characteristics and actions necessary to remedy; all through a proper discernment and discrimination.

As an example, **we may react hastily to a confrontation because we didn't stop to recognize what was really being done (or undone).** Instead of being prepared proactively, we respond reactively. It's like trying to foresee and control a reflex reaction. Now, if we could do that, we wouldn't need our reflexes. We have to see what's coming, and we have to know how to handle it.

It's no different than a baseball player trying to recognize the pitches. If he sees it in time to respond and adjust accordingly, the chances of success skyrocket. If he doesn't recognize it in time, his chances drop dramatically. Just look at the results of the Houston Astros cheating scandal of 2017. In this pathetic scheme, the Astro's strategically placed a lookout where the spotter could read (steal) the signals of the desired pitch being sent from the catcher to the pitcher. The "sign-stealer" would then relay the information to someone in the dugout. If the pitch was to be a fastball, the person would bang on a something like an old garbage can lid to signal the batter that a heater was coming. This allowed the batter to zero in on the fastball which overwhelming increased their odds of getting a hit. The result, the Astro's stole a world series.

Now, this doesn't lend well to the old adage that says, "Cheaters never prosper." In this case, the Astro's did "prosper" because they walked away as world champions. They proudly dawned the fancy diamond rings and carried home a tainted world series trophy. Yet for them, they are weakened, tarnished, and forever known as cheaters. Not something most rational people would want to hang over their heads for the rest of their lives.

They prospered in earthly things, forgoing moral and heavenly ways. Will they come to regret it later, even admitting truth and showing remorse? Some maybe. But only a person's actions will answer such questions. Judas Iscariot felt remorse but never repented (Matthew 27:3-4). He desperately tried to unwind his betrayal, but there is no record of him seeking or

147

showing repentance. He panicked for a way out, not for forgiveness (Matthew 27:5).

But yes, having foreknowledge and access to more information absolutely makes a difference. If you know what's coming, you have a better chance of handling it. They knew what was coming, and they were successful in the moment because of it. But in the end game, the "championship" of Houston Astros of 2017 will simply be another asterisk mark in the record books; a note to highlight their "achievement" in true failing fashion.

Again, **reacting hastily to situations without knowing the full picture only magnifies the opportunity to mess things up.** Whether intentional or not, the results of quick judgements lend to reactionary responses as opposed to proactive actions. We need to develop and refine our skills of awareness and discernment. Acting in reckless haste usually leaves a wake of damage in its aftermath.

Think of a young boy who waits for dad to come home from work so they can play catch with the brand-new baseball glove he just got for his birthday. Now, dad's had an unusually rough day and just wants to get home and unwind in the chair, maybe catch the end of the game and get his mind off the rotten day he's had. His boy is outside in the front yard, fully excited and eagerly waiting for him to drive around the corner, quickly drop everything, and play catch. He just can't wait! It's been the only thing his son can think of since he put that new mitt on. For him, 5 o'clock couldn't come any sooner!

Dad rounds the corner and drives in a little hot, screeches the brakes, gets out, slams the door on his finger, and angrily mutters inaudibles as he plows-pavement towards the front door. His boy hesitates, but just can't help it, and he eventually asks, "Hey Dad, you ready to play catch now...you said you would, remember?"

Dad loses it like Vesuvius...but only until he sees the tears start to slowly roll down his boy's face. Dad knows he blew it, but far too proud to walk it back. He continues without pause and simply storms into the unexpecting house. It only continues from there. Eventually, yelling, disputes, anger, frustration, separation, and fresh scars that grow to remain. Days then turn into the *war with silent swords* - Not a good response.

It sounds childlike, even puerile, but like the example above, **there are many times people fail to realize they are even under attack.** Whether by indifference, clouded emotions, or extenuating circumstances, far too many times we just don't see the assault coming and fail to recognize it for what it is – an attack. Even worse, we get calloused into a tolerance that dims our ability to discern properly or accurately when it's right before us. The Lord knows how easily we forgo our most basic instincts and seem willing to gravitate to the perceptive ease of spiritual blindness (Psalm 115:4-8; Jeremiah 5:21, Ezekiel 12:2).

Goes without saying that it's hard to see something when you don't expect it or are intentionally conditioned to ignore it. Satan loves our human naiveness and uses it against us. Again, it's been that way since Eden and the temptations that condemned the man and the woman.

Satan is cunning and separating, dressed in the elegance of temptation's alure, and he's a master craftsman at it. He wants to wound with evil and ever-lasting effects. If we do not recognize we are being attacked, we can't formulate a strong defense, and we surely cannot position a counterattack. It just isn't going to work. We must have *eyes that see* and *ears that hear* so we can understand what is before us, and how to navigate through it (Proverbs 20:12; Matthew 11:15, 13:9, 43, Luke 10:23, 14:35; Revelation 2:7, 11, 17, 29, 3:6, 13, 22, 13:9).

Even if we don't see spiritual attacks coming, we can still have a plan to thwart them! Our approach to how we handle our attacks are predicated by the delicate nature of our current and underlining attitudes. Even our worldview comes into play. If we are accustomed to employing the Fruits of the Spirit, our responses are coupled with the blessings of their intent. We are reminded to bear good-fruit because, "…against such things there is no law" (Galatians 5:22-23). In other words, nothing can stop us when we are armored-up with God's panoply and wielding a full spectrum of the Fruits of the Spirit.

Equally, **our knowledgebase of Scripture is paramount to our capabilities in traversing the most dangerous of life's mountains, especially those littered with spiritual attacks.** We know through compassionate and straightforward statements from Jesus Himself, that life for a follower of Christ would be fraught with persecution and hate (John 15:18). Yet fully knowing this, He also provided hope:

Jesus spoke to the people once more and said, "I am the light of the world. If you follow me, you won't have to walk in darkness, because you will have the light that leads to life."
John 8:12 (NLT)

Jesus seeks our faithful walk with Him to be the spirit of our defensive capabilities. He taught that our defense must be fueled by a firm foundation of Scripture and the wisdom to rely upon it. It's the confidence to withstand the attack because you know you have the best and only defense to defeat it. There should be no uncertainties. No wavering. You can have confidence if you are readied and equipped properly within all the facets of God's Armor (Ephesians 6:13-17). It's the reason He gave them. And He graciously unveiled their specific use, leaving no chance at misuse or some form of misapplication.

151

Again, did you notice that within the Armor of God, there is only one offensive weapon? As mentioned earlier, if this didn't necessarily standout to you before, it's time to go take a closer look (again, Ephesians 6:13-17). Be like the Bereans and search the Scriptures yourself (Acts 17:11). Yes, while most writers would provide the passage specific for your reference, for this one, I hope you grab a Bible now... and don't come back. Drop this and go look. Slow the Scriptures down with intentionality, and you'll see the Holy Spirit continue to bring illuminating light that shows the infinite perfection of God's revelation to us – The Word.

Sure, I want you to finish this book, but the Book I'm sending you to now is the one you can't live without – The Bible! And it's perfectly fine if you stay there and keep reading. This will be here when you get back...

Now, go read Ephesians 6:10-18. Learn the facets and intricacies of the equipment He's provided

– The blessed Armor of God!

In addition to all this, take up the shield of faith,

with which you can extinguish

all the flaming arrows of the evil one.

Ephesians 6:16 (NIV)

Chapter 15 –It's not WWJD…
It's *What Did Jesus Teach?*

We can defend the fiery arrows of our enemies effectively if we know and apply what has been taught by **Jesus Christ.** He exampled this through His responses to the temptations in the Judean wilderness (Matthew 4:1-11; Mark 1:12-13; Luke 4:1-13). Although there are only three specifically recorded temptations, our Lord was constantly being tempted throughout those 40-days. The Scripture states

Jesus was there, "for forty days, being tempted by the devil." (Luke 4:2). Now, although there were only three recorded temptations, it was enough of an example to show us the best way to defeat the sinful lures (and people) of this world.

Jesus gave us <u>the</u> teaching to respond to all temptations – Scripture, Scripture, Scripture! – From the first recorded temptation (Matthew 4:3-4, answered with Deuteronomy 8:3), the second (Matthew 4:5-7, answered with Deuteronomy 6:16), and the third (Matthew 4:8-10, answered from Deuteronomy 6:12-13), Jesus gave us the defense plan. And it should be no surprise that Satan employed the same tactics with Jesus that he did with Eve and Adam by twisting words and meanings in hopes of tripping Him up. Jesus is the Word (John 1:1), which made Satan's attempts foolishly futile, dare I say stupid. But for us, this is a teaching to heed carefully.

We know that **Scripture is the best way to defend against temptation and sin, so use it!** If you are feeling lured into wrongdoing, if you're being drawn to lusts, if you are sensing an impulse to give in to the traps of temptation - immediately go pick up the Bible and hold it as tight as you can to your chest! You don't have to open it (yet). Just clench it with everything you have and be like Paul; say over and over – *Your grace is enough. Your grace is enough. Your grace is enough.*

I'm going to be intentionally blunt. I don't know any believer in Christ that can consider giving in to such sins as drug and alcohol abuse, pornography, or adultery, when gripping a Bible in their hands. If you have trouble with such temptations, you need to carry a Bible at all times. Again, it doesn't need to be opened, but the sheer power of holding God's Word so tightly to yourself will give you great strength to master any sin.

Pray for Satan to be rebuked in the Name of Jesus Christ of Nazareth, and you'll be spiritually positioned to thwart anything Satan tries. Then, when the temptation has passed, open the Bible, maybe to Psalms or your favorite passage, and thank the Lord for watching over you as the Good Shepherd. You were pulled back by the Shepherds crook[32], and now you're positioned to walk again. The Word of God cannot be overcome and can never be defeated. Walk <u>with</u> the Word and walk <u>in</u> the Word. The Bible is the best spiritual GPS you'll ever need.

Satan does a lot to stir things up. He throws a subtle little curve ball, and often we bite just swinging for the fences. Seeing the results in all kinds of problems and chaos, he then steps back and says, *that was sure easy.* We need to stop affording him the opening and maintain our focus to live righteously. It is so important to stay with the spiritual guardrails the Lord provides. Sometimes we make it too easy to be preyed upon, even inviting to such attentions and exposures.

Remember, **a sharp and sober mind can discern even the craftiest of dressings.** With the truthful clarity of Scripture, we can clearly distinguish the wolf through the guise of sheepskin (Matthew 7:14). It's no different than striking a single match in a completely darkened room. Immediately all things present come to light. Nothing is hidden…all is revealed.

But again, **in order to use the Scriptures, we need to know and understand the Scriptures.** It's not the *addresses* of Scripture that's most important, rather the content in application and affirmations to ourselves and others. We can't respond properly to situations if we don't know what to respond with. This takes time, coupled with a devote dedication to sources that provide our daily bread and nurturing. Yes Lord, give us this day…(Matthew 6:11).

Maybe you have heard the term "Sola Scriptura?" This is Latin for 'Scripture alone' which refers to a Reformed Christian theological doctrine that is generally held by many (if not most) Protestant Christian denominations today. MacArthur explains, "Sola Scriptura meant that the Bible was the only divinely revealed Word and therefore the believer's true authority for sound doctrine and righteous living."[33] Thus, in sum, the Bible is the final authority. Though not to be academically outlaid here, the essence is that Scripture alone (the Bible) is inerrant, infallible, and historically accurate. I firmly agree and support its foundations as well. It's the final Word in all matters.

In a similar context to sola Scriptura, have you ever thought what it would be like if the only language spoken was solely Scripture? Really, to have the only spoken interactions between mankind to be verses would be such a welcomed change to the filth that spues far too often now. To be bound to only Scripture in conversations seems limiting, but it really is something to experience. I have, and it is poetically special.

While co-leading a tour in Israel, we gathered early in our hotel lobby to coordinate the upcoming logistics and destinations for our group that day. Convening in this rather small and titchy foyer, we noticed another band of visitors also preparing their day. It was a smaller group made up of elderly men and woman, most of whom were probably north of seventy to eighty years in age. The women were sitting, engaged in quite subtle musings, and the men were standing aside in a makeshift-type circle. Drawing closer to them, my radar instantly went buzzing – they're talking Scripture! My wife Kim came closer and noticed I was fully engaged in the eavesdropping on their conversation. In truth, I really wasn't making any effort to hid it. Tugging my shirt, she finally got my attention. I turned my head, but kept my eyes and ears locked-in. Leaning over while cupping my hand to the side of my mouth, I whispered, "quiet…just listen to them. They're only speaking in Scripture!" And it wasn't just verses here and there interspersed within their conversation. It was nothing but Scripture.

The conversation had a real divine harmony about it. It didn't surprise me as much as it delighted me. This small group of righteous elderly people were engaged in genuine conversations that were just Scripture. One would say, "Ah yes, but thus saith the Lord…" Then another, "Yes, Yes, indeed, the prophet Jeremiah reminded us that…" And then another, "Oh, but remember, a thousand years is only but a day to the Lord…" It was just Scripture, answered with Scripture, supported by Scripture, agreed as Scripture, and loved as Scripture. It was beautiful…so pure and so righteous.

They were such an inspirational example of good and faithful servants. Dare I say, it was better than morning orange juice from Israel. Interestingly, I did later find out they were from Texas *(Don't know why I'm adding that, other than I'm guessing it will mean something to someone).*

But again, with Scripture, it's not the gift of oration as much as it is the content of the oration itself (i.e. Moses and Aaron). We are called to not only be ready with an answer for the hope that we have (1 Peter 3:15), but to treasure the gift of the answers themselves. In remembrance of that small little band of righteous believers whose witness was a moment to treasure:

Let the message of Christ dwell among you richly as you teach and admonish one another with all wisdom through psalms, hymns, and songs from the Spirit, singing to God with gratitude in your hearts.

Colossians 3:16 (NIV)

Looking at their example, the use of Scripture seemed to be the only thing they needed to find joy and purpose to their days. Many may not possess this level of biblical expertise and acumen, but it can be achieved. Day-to-day memory verses, daily bread calendars, personal study devotions, Bible-in-a-year, and proper worship music are all great ingredients to well round your daily spiritual multi-vitamins. While this can be difficult with daily time constraints, even a little will go a long way. Slow down and make the time for spiritual nourishment.

In days where we find ourselves struggling for time and ability to engage with the Lord as we hope to, we can pause for prayer and seek some interceding. In fact, **we know we can trust the Holy Spirit to intervene when we acknowledge we need the assist**. Even more so when we don't recognize it. Remember Paul's encouragement:

In the same way, the Spirit helps us in our weakness. We do not know what we ought to pray for, but the Spirit himself intercedes for us through wordless groans. And He who searches our hearts knows the mind of the Spirit, because the Spirit intercedes for God's people in accordance with the will

161

of God. And we know that in all things God works for the good of those who love Him, who have been called according to His purpose.

Romans 8:26-28 (NIV)

Throughout it all, **don't worry if you are temporarily wounded and need to be carried or crooked back to the flock.** It may be for your own good. And just like many parents used say before the correction of punishment landed, "This is gonna hurt me more than it hurts you." Jesus loves His sheep, and He wants us to depend on Him. But let the dependance hinge upon our mistakes and shortcomings, not the necessity of a divine discipline. Learn to call upon the Lord and seek His understandings and forgo giving a second thought to your own.

As for me, I shall call upon God,
And the LORD will save me.

Psalms 55:16

Remember, we were given to Jesus by the Father (John 3:35), and He wants to return us better than He found us. So, the appreciation to walk and not be carried grows as we become Christ-like and worthy of Kingdom service. We need a craved yearning to hunger and thirst for righteousness (Matt 5:6), confident in the return of fruitful works of faith, hope, and love.

But in the mire of hardships, He wants us to yield our burdens to Him and know He is always there – always with us. He will always be with us, just as we will always be with Him **(Psalm 73:23;** Matthew 28:20).

The psalm offerings of David gives us many examples of bearing our burdens in the affordance of the Lord's sustaining power and protections. It's a character quality that's consistent throughout his prayers. And if anyone could raise testimony to the weight of heavy trials and tribulations (and the need for several good escape plans), it was David!

The plea:

For my iniquities are gone over my head; As a heavy burden they weigh too much for me.

    ~ Psalm 38:4

The response:

Cast your burden upon the LORD and He will sustain you; He will never allow the righteous to be shaken. ~ Psalm 55:22

Blessed be the Lord, who daily bears our burden, The God who is our salvation. Selah.

    ~ Psalm 68:19

Escape Route – En Gedi

Waterfall - En Ged

Photos by J. Young

Trust in the LORD and do good;

dwell in the land and enjoy safe pasture.

Psalm 37:3 (NIV)

Chapter 16 - Out to Pasture, Into the Sunset...

Coursing through life is not easy, nor was it meant to be, especially for those who seek the sheepfold of our Good Shepherd. Jesus has given us many assurances that are meant to guide us through those darkened valleys. Yes, even the valley of death (Psa 23:4). As His followers, we need to embrace the undertakings and opportunities He places before us. Whether testing, teaching, waiting, or watching doors close while others swing open, we can have the unshakeable confidence to know He is always watching over us...

Blessed be the LORD,
Because He has heard the voice of my supplication.
The LORD is my strength and my shield;
My heart trusts in Him, and I am helped;
Therefore my heart exults,
And with my song I shall thank Him.
The LORD is their strength,
And He is a saving defense to His anointed.
Save Your people and bless Your inheritance;
Be their shepherd also, and carry them forever.
Psalm 28:6~9

One of my most treasured places in all the world is located on the sloping hillsides in the northern part of the Galilee in Israel. It's a small, pleasing little horse ranch that sits above the Sea of Galilee (also called: Sea of Tiberias, Lake Tiberias, Lake of Gennesaret, Kinneret, and others) on the northeastern slopes that feed into the Jordan Valley.

Vered Hagalil is a lodging retreat that's nestled just a few earshot's away from the Mount of Beatitudes where our Lord Jesus gave His treasured *Sermon on the Mount*. It has an incredible viewing-point overlooking Capernaum, Tabgha (the site of John 21: the Miraculous Catch of Fish), Ginosar, and Tiberias. From here, you can also see Mount Arbel which is where Jesus is believed to have given The Great Commission to the Talmidim[34] (Matthew 28:16-20; Mark 16:14-18; Luke 24:36-49; John 20:19-23; Acts 1:6-8). The region is filled with so much biblical history, it would take pages and pages to reference and cross-reference.

The appeal to Vered Hagalil is its serene setting that fully avails the spectacular beauty of the Sea of Galilee. Something no panoramic picture can do justice to, and surely nothing that can be written here. You must see it in person to fully appreciate why our Lord Jesus spent so much time here.

The drawing to this place of rest and tranquility in the hills of the Galilee are easily tied to the reasons Jesus so often withdrew here to pray (Matthew 14:13, 22; Mark 1:35, 45; 3:13; Luke 6:12-13). Spurgeon remarked specifically regarding the suitability of these separations and this particular location itself stating, "Jesus, therefore, to prevent interruption, to give Himself the opportunity of pouring out His whole soul, and to avoid ostentation, sought the mountain."[35]

The Lord was giving us another example of the best ways to formulate and structure our times with the Father. He was teaching us to be persistent and intentional with our worship, devotions, and most specifically, our prayers (1 Thessalonians 5:17). In the inviting hills of the Galilee, you can easily appreciate a different type of isolation while feeling a complete sense of presence. Sounds conflicting on the surface, but it truly is the only way to describe something that is indescribable, especially to someone who hasn't felt it. Here, you can isolate yourself from worldly consternations and seek the peace of God's pasture in ways He intended so long ago. (Psalm 37:3; 79:13; 95:7; 100:3; Jeremiah 23:3; 50:19; Ezekiel 34:13-14, 31; Micah. 2:12; Zephaniah 2:17; John 10:9).

I too find it a perfect place to humble oneself into a privately secluded condition that allows a unique clarity to hear the Holy Spirit, unabated by our chaotic and worldly interruptions. It's a place that brokenness, confusion, and uncertainty can be treated with the calming and assuring presence of an Ever-Loving Shepherd. When you are there, it is easy to appreciate why He choose this as His primary place to be alone with the Father. Again, I'm compelled the same…

The hills of the Galilee are also an inviting place to offer and embrace worship to our Lord and Savior Jesus Christ. There is such a spiritual presence when you're in the Land and I always feel a desire to outpour psalms and prayers when taking respite there. It's a gripping stimulus that arouses (even requires) some form of a response. It equally resonates a stirring to welcome such spiritual humilities. Whether scribing devotions, laments, or just psalms of praise, its welcoming to become spiritually emersed in some form of engagement with the Lord while in the Land. And what's specially unique is that everyone has a different form of reaction and response. As a homage to such moments, one such writing is offered the end of this chapter. The hope is to be able to paint even a fracture of the picture for those who have never gazed upon the precious vistas where our Messiah spent most His earthly life – The Galilee. *(Authors note: The psalm offering was done while in the Galilee, just after Israel was re-opened following the Covid-19 pandemic of 2019).*

It is a continual prayer for all who are drawn to explore Israel to make the intentional "ask" of the Lord. When we were first invited to go by our close friend Pastor Tod Hornby, I mocked the opportunity. It was easy to start unfolding a response laced with excuses layered upon excuses. Things I thought were real hindrances and problematic came right to the forefront of the conversation without pause. I was ready with the wrong answers.

When I hung up the phone, comfortable that the request was impossible, the Holy Spirit gave an immediate rebuking. I didn't even ask permission or provision by carelessly casting it aside so quickly, and I was heavily admonished because of it. The lesson here is - don't forgo the asking. I learned, and it has made waves ever since! So herein is my prayer for all who have not made the pilgrimage to Israel...

Heavenly Father, Lord God, our Savior and Good Shepherd: I pray for any and all that open this book that haven't had the chance to have a revealing of Israel and an engagement with Your people, that You Lord would open their heart to the desire, and the door of opportunity. – In Jesus Name, Amen

Our Lord inclines His ear when we seek the calming of His gracious and ever-faithful voice (Psalm 10:17; 17:6; 31:1-5; 71:1-6; 86:1-7). He's attentively aware of all things and desires to be intrinsically involved in all we do (John 21:17). This means He is engaged in the good undertakings of our daily efforts and watches carefully over the bad. He always has been (Isaiah 41:10, Jeremiah 1:8, 19, 15:20, Matthew 28:20). Within grace and mercy, He faithfully waits upon our responses when we fail and fall sort. He carries us when we are wounded and rejoices when we return to walking again. David affirms, "Save Your people and bless Your inheritance; be their shepherd and carry them forever." (Psalm 28:9 NIV)

When we hit the pitfalls or face things too hard to bear, it is not hard to remember He is always with us. His hope though, is that we strive to walk again, bearing His banner in boldness and truth. Listen to the Voice of Truth, and do not be afraid. He is ever-present with the broadest of shoulders to bear us lest we hit the spiritual guardrails and need that repair only the Lord can provide.

Our Good Shepherd will never let us stray, but it might hurt a little when we are oblivious and need a restoration of healing; one that only the Hand of grace and mercy can provide. Just remember the picture of the Ever-loving Shepherd and the small lamb, and you will know He is eternally with you…

WRITTEN UNDER HIS GRACE — 2024/25

AMEN

RETURN TO GOD'S PASTURE (THE GALILEE, 2020)

O' LORD OF ARMS-WIDE,

GRACIOUS ADONAI, LONG HAS IT BEEN SINCE TIMES IN YOUR PASTURE...
>THE MOUNTAINS AND HILLS SURROUNDING,
>THE AIR FILLING,
>THE LAND RISING,
>THE SUN SETTING,
>THE GALILEE GLISTENS ANEW,

SHALOM UPON SHALOM...

YESHUA, LONG HAS IT BEEN SINCE WE'VE STOOD WELCOMED TO YOUR REFUGE...
>YOUR CITY DONNED A CLOTH DUSTED; WRITHING FOR AIR.
>YOUR DOORS SHUT CERTAIN; THE SEPARATION GREW.
>YOUR GATES MOURNED-TIGHT; WE IMPORTUNED HOPE.
>YOUR GAZE YET TURNED; WE MACHINATED A RETURN.
>YOUR ATTENTIONS INCLINED; WE UPRAISED OUR FAITH.

CAST US REPAIR...OUR RETURN TO THE HOME...

LORD, LONG HAS IT BEEN SINCE EMBRACING YOUR LAND...
>YOU MEASURED, WE PRAYED.
>YOU LONGED, WE LONGED TOO.
>YOU CALLED, WE LISTENED.
>YOU TUGGED, WE THEN FOLLOWED.
>YOU INVITED, WE REJOICED!

ENGAGING UPON REVEALING...

NOT LONG NOW, THOUGH IT HAS BEEN SOME TIME...
>YOU CAST AWAY DARK CLOUDS; YOU WASHED THE YOUNG FACES.
>YOU BATHED THE LAND; YOU CLEANSED ITS STONES.
>YOU RAISED NEW COLORS; YOU YIELDED ROOM.
>YOU ABATED SHARP THORNS; YOU WHISPERED, "IT IS TIME!"
>YOU OUTSTRETCHED HANDS; YOU BESEECHED...AWAITING PRAISE.

RETURN UNTO ME, MY SHEEP, YOU KNOW MY VOICE!
>YES, MINE IS THE VOICE OF UNFAILING LOVE.
>FOR I ALSO LONG YOUR RETURN UNTO ME.

>I, YOUR SHEPHERD, AWAIT YOUR DANCING!
>I, YOUR KING, AWAIT YOUR SONG!
>I, YOUR SAVIOR, AWAIT YOUR WORSHIP!
>AND I, THE BEGOTTEN, AWAIT YOUR LOVE.

LISTEN TO ME NOW, AND RETURN UNTO ME...FOR I HAVE PREPARED FOR YOU...

A HOME UPON HOME!

At The Southern Steps – Jerusalem, Israel
31.77564° N 35.234734° E

Kim worshiping at Vered Hagalil, Chorazim
(Mt. of Beatitudes in the background)

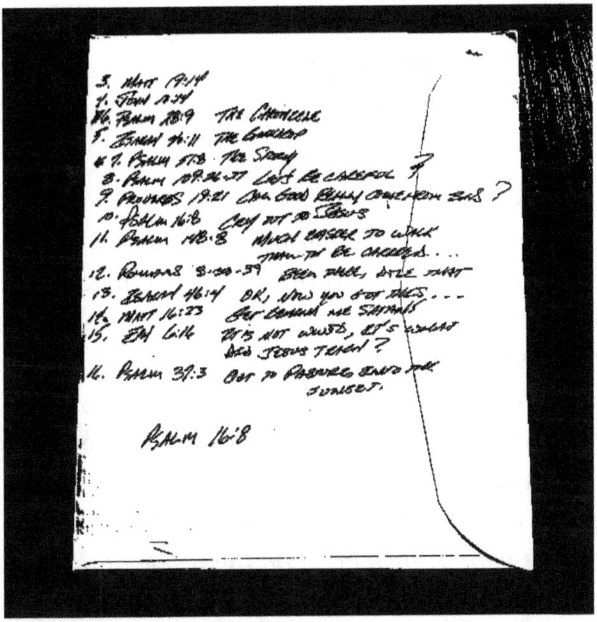

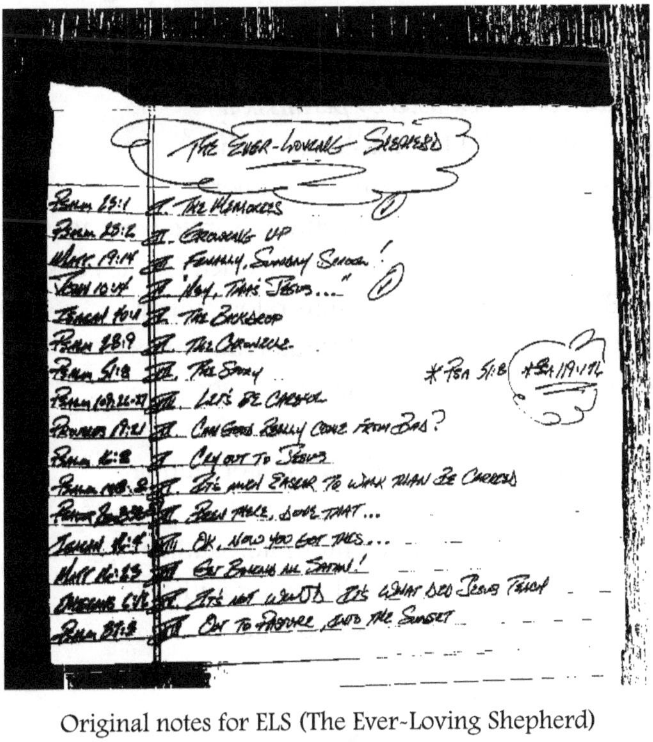

Original notes for ELS (The Ever-Loving Shepherd)

Chapter Illustrations

Chapter 1 [Psalm 32:1] – Illustrator: author

Chapter 2 [Psalm 23:2] – Illustrator: author

Chapter 3 [Matthew 19:14] – Illustrator: author

Chapter 4 [John 10:14] – This is a photo of a tattoo imprint taken from a stone that is circa 400-years old. This was received from Wassim Razzouk, 27th generation family artist and kind friend. It is one of many used by Razzouk Tattoo in the Old City of Jerusalem (and now, around the world). "The art has been in the family for 700 hundred years starting in Egypt, when the family started tattooing pilgrims for a living. *"Our ancestors used tattoos to mark Christian Copts in Egypt with a small cross on the inside of the wrist to grant them access to churches. Those without it would have difficulty entering the church; therefore, and from a very young age (sometimes even a few months old) Christians would tattoo their children with the cross identifying them as Copts."* – Razzouk Tattoo (Jerusalem, Israel) Since 1300 A.D. *used by permission*

Chapter 5 [Isaiah 40:11] – Illustrator: author

Chapter 6 [Psalm 28:9] – Illustrator: author

Chapter 7 [Psalm 119:176] – Illustrator is from Bangladesh; remains anonymous. This was the first picture created for the book.

Chapter 8 [Psalm 109:26-27] – Illustrator: author

Chapter 9 [Proverbs 19:21] – Illustrator: author

Chapter 10 [Psalm 16:8] – Illustrator: author

Chapter 11 [Psalm 148:8] – Illustrator: author

Chapter 12 [Romans 8:38-39] – Illustrator: author

Chapter 13 [Isaiah 46:4] – Illustrator: author

Chapter 14 [Matthew 16:23] – Illustrator: author

Chapter 15 [Ephesians 6:16] – Illustrator: author

Chapter 16 [Psalm 37:3] – Illustrator: author

Notes:

---

[1] True ordination (the setting aside) is not obtained via 24-hour internet application and certificate to follow through some fast and easy process (i.e. The Universal Life Church). Rev. Young is ordained through the Evangelical Church Alliance; One of the longest-standing credible ordination bodies in the United States established in 1887.
https://www.ecainternational.org/history

[2] Clarification – Ecclesiastes 5:14, the New English Translation, or NET version, interchanges the word "luck" for "evil travail"; KJV, "misfortune"; NKJV, NIV, "bad venture"; ESB, CSB, and "bad investment"; NASB. The NET is the only version to have this word usage.

[3] Hebrew: priest

[4] The combination of dramatically and drastically

[5] UNESCO World Heritage Convention. (n.d.). Baptism Site "Bethany Beyond the Jordan" (Al-Maghtas). Retrieved December 30th, 2024, from
https://whc.unesco.org/en/list/1446/

[6] SeetheHolyLand.net (n.d.). Church of Saint Peter in Gallicantu. Retrieved December 30th, 2024, from https://www.seetheholyland.net/church-of-st-peter-in-gallicantu/

[7] Christians United for Israel (July 19, 2019). News. Retrieved Jan 3rd, 2025 from https://www.cufi.org.uk/news/when-neil-armstrong-walked-on-jerusalem-i-am-more-excited-stepping-on-these-stones-than-stepping-on-the-moon-2/

[8] "Christ in the Garden of Gethsemane" by German painter, Heinrich Hofmann (1886).

[9] This is a new shoot growing from the base of an ancient olive tree in the garden of Gethsemane (see Isa 11:1).

[10] Northview Bible Church was a church plant from Fourth Memorial Church in Spokane, WA., during the early 70's. The Young's were one of many original families. The first gatherings were at a Pizza Parlor called Cicero's Pizza & Steakhouse, later Savage House Pizza.

[11] The MDA telethon was yearly television broadcast that ran from 1966 to 2014. Jerry Lewis (a famous actor/comedian) hosted what started as 24-hour event that would raise millions of dollars for people affected by the dreadful disease of muscular dystrophy.

[12] The original Fairwood Shopping Center was located near Mead High School. It included stores like Albertsons Grocery, and Giant T, Radio Shack, Zips, Stockyards Inn North, the Jean Hause (famous for a pair of jeans that could fit King Kong), and Savage House Pizza (also the home of our church plant).

[13] "It's like a lion and a tiger mixed... bred for its skills in magic."

[14] Pong was one of the first computer games ever created. The game was originally developed by Allan Alcorn and released in 1972 by Atari corporations.

[15] John Lee Hooker, 1948.

[16] Blank music paper used by composers to place notes on.

[17] Spirit of '76 (aka: Yankee Doodle) Painting by Archibald Willard (circa 1875). Public Domain, https://commons.wikimedia.org/w/index.php?curid=499045

[18] Wikipedia contributors. (2024, October 30). Footprints (poem). In *Wikipedia, The Free Encyclopedia*. Retrieved 18:33, November 15, 2024, from https://en.wikipedia.org/w/index.php?title=Footprints_(poem)&oldid=1254299963

[19] Hebrew word for the first Five Books of the Moses (Genesis, Exodus, Leviticus, Numbers, and Deuteronomy)

[20] https://www.christianforums.com/threads/did-shepherds-really-break-a-lambs-leg-on-purpose.3295088/

[21] Lee, G., Lifeson, A., Peart, N. (1980). Freewill [Rush]. On *Permanent Waves*. Mercury Records.

[22] Aka: domestic ass

[23] Azarova, M., (2023, May 21). *The Hawthorne Effect or Observer Bias in User Research*. Nielsen Norman Group.

https://www.nngroup.com/articles/hawthorne-effect-observer-bias-user-research/

[24] The jolly Jewish holiday of Purim commemorates the (Divinely orchestrated) salvation of the Jewish people in the ancient Persian empire from Haman's plot "to destroy, kill and annihilate all the Jews..." – Chabbad.org
https://www.chabad.org/holidays/purim/article_cdo/aid/645309/jewish/What-Is-Purim.htm

[25] Spurgeon, C. (5 Dec 2016). Psalm 88 by C. H. Spurgeon. Retrieved from
https://www.blueletterbible.org/Comm/spurgeon_charles/tod/ps088.cfm

[26] Lexicon, Blue Letter Bible, Lexicon, Strong's H270.
https://www.blueletterbible.org/lexicon/h270/nasb95/wlc/0-1/, Nov. 12 ,2024.

[27] "The midrash is a repository of rabbinic wisdom, storytelling, and tradition—often couched within the verses of scripture, which the rabbis mine for layer upon layer of hidden meaning." – Chabad.org
"An ancient commentary on part of the Hebrew scriptures, attached to the biblical text." – Britannica.com

[28] The Lubavitcher Rebbe, Chabad.org.
https://www.chabad.org/parshah/in-depth/default_cdo/aid/35880/jewish/Vayigash-In-Depth.htm, Dec. 13th, 2024.

[29] The Lubavitcher Rebbe, Chabad.org.
https://www.chabad.org/parshah/in-depth/default_cdo/aid/35880/jewish/Vayigash-In-Depth.htm, Dec. 13th, 2024.

[30] Guzik, D. (6/2022). Study Guide for Genesis 3 by David Guzik. Retrieved from https://www.blueletterbible.org/comm/guzik_david/study-guide/genesis/genesis-3.cfm

[31] Hebrew: mother and father

[32] The crook walking stick has been an essential companion to farmers and shepherds around the world for thousands of years. They've been used as a way tool to herd sheep, to provide stability on hilly ground, to hang a

lantern on dark mornings, or even for defense from predators – The History of Shepherd's Crooks https://www.walkingsticks.co.uk/blog/the-history-of-shepherds-crooks.html, Jan. 12th, 2025.

[33] MacArthur, J. (1/2023). Why Does Sola Scriptura Still Matter? Retrieved from https://www.gty.org/library/blog/B160722/why-does-sola-scriptura-still-matter, Jan 19th, 2025.

[34] Hebrew for disciples (plural)

[35] Spurgeon, Charles Haddon "The New Park Street Pulpit" Volumes 1-6 and "The Metropolitan Tabernacle Pulpit" Volumes 7-63 (Pasadena, Texas: Pilgrim Publications, 1990).

About the Author

Born in Long Beach, California, John migrated with his family to Spokane, Washington in 1972. Growing up and later settling in North Idaho, he attended Liberty University, graduating in 2011 with an A.A. degree in Religion (Honors) and then again in 2013 with a B.S. Degree (Summa Cum Laude) in Interdisciplinary Studies with cognates in Biblical Studies, Business Administration, and Theology. John was then ordained by the Evangelical Church Alliance in February of 2015.

Since 2008, Rev. Young has served as the executive director and pastor of CornerStone Christian Ministries and CornerStone Christian Academy in Post Falls, Idaho. He met his wife Kimberly just prior to acquiring stewardship of the school in May of that year. This is where their ministry started. They were married on the playground in front of the entire school under the guise of a "fire-drill" in September of 2008.

Over his years of ministry service, he has taught and preached with a passion that has reached hundreds of students and families alike. He has a strong passion for Israel and loves teaching in the Holy Land which has inspired many of his writings, including *Psalms of the Small Lamb* & *The Spiritual Guardrails (2026)*. He is also the author of the children's books series, *Sometimes Solomon: Sometimes a Dog is just a Dog* & *Sometimes Solomon and the Onkey Donkeys (2025)*.

www.ingramcontent.com/pod-product-compliance
Lightning Source LLC
Chambersburg PA
CBHW071529040426
42452CB00008B/940